THE TWELVE SONS OF ISRAEL

THE TWELVE SONS OF ISRAEL

Compiled by

Dr. Norman L. Heap

CALIFORNIA PUBLISHING CO.
San Francisco

FIRST EDITION

All rights reserved, including the right of reproduction in whole or in part in any form.

Copyright © 1988 by Dr. Norman L. Heap

Published by Family History Publications
2226 Oakgrove Road #343
Walnut Creek, CA 94598

Manufactured in the United States of America
ISBN: 0-945905-04-1

Dedication

To the sons of Israel and their descendants who faithfully kept the records from which the Holy Scriptures are derived, and from whom prophets of the living God are descended, including but not limited to, Moses, Aaron, Joshua, Daniel, Isaiah, Ezekiel, Elijah, Malachi, Lehi, Nephi, Mosiah, Benjamin, Abinadi, Alma, Helaman, Mormon, Moroni, Joseph Smith and Ezra Taft Benson, and most importantly to Messiah, the Son of Man and the Son of God, who will save the world for the sins of its people on condition of their repentance.

Acknowledgements

Translations of the Holy Scriptures are generally in public domain. Nonetheless, the compiler gratefully acknowledges The Jewish Publication Society of America, The Church of Jesus Christ of Latter Days Saints, and The Reorganized Church of Jesus Christ of Latter Day Saints for quotations used from their respective copyrighted scriptures.

Grateful acknowledgement is given to the J.H. Parry Company for extensive use of the Book of Jasher which was translated from the original Hebrew into English, published in 1887 and reprinted in 1973. Other copyrighted material is used by permission and courtesy of several publishers. Their works are listed in a bibliography. Special thanks to The Jewish Publication Society, Doubleday and Company, World Bible Publishers and Kregel Publications for the use of selected quotations from the works listed. The compiler is most grateful for an understanding companion and wife, Virginia Thayer. Without her this book would not be possible.

Prologue

Abraham and Isaac were the great-grandfather and grandfather respectively, of the twelve sons of Israel. We have learned from studying their lives that Abraham, Isaac, and Israel were friends, servants and prophets of God. They, along with the rest of us, existed as spirits in the pre-mortal world before being born in the flesh.

We also learned from a previous work entitled *Abraham, Isaac, and Jacob, Servants and Prophets of God*, that Jehovah (Yahweh) is the living God of planet earth, which He created under the direction of His Father (Elohim). Life on earth represents a second stage of existence for human beings. Those who come to earth and take physical bodies have qualified to do so by the choices they made and the lives they lived while they were spirits in the pre-mortal world. Some spirits are greater than others, and Jehovah (Yahweh) is the greatest of them all. Each is the spiritual son or daughter of God, the Eternal Father (Elohim).

The purposes of God are to bring to pass the immortality and eternal life of men and women. The purpose of earth life is to prove each soul to see if he or she will do all that has been commanded of him or her, thereby qualifying each for eternal life.

God has chosen to work through a covenant people to achieve His purposes. The covenant people through whom the Lord God Jehovah (Yahweh) works had their origins in Noah, Shem, and Eber, but came into fruition through Abraham, Isaac, Israel and their posterity, particularly through the sons of Israel.

The Lord God will intervene in the lives of men and women as required to achieve His purposes and to bless them as needed, but He will not pre-empt any man or woman's agency to choose or force him or her to do good or evil.

Without memory of the pre-mortal world, and walking by faith, men and women are free to obey God's commandments and reap the consequences in benefits and blessings. Men and women are also free to sin against God's commandments and reap the consequences in anguish, guilt, sorrow, pain, and denials of God's blessings. Sin is overcome only through complete repentance and His forgiveness. He hears and answers the prayers of those who fervently, sincerely, truly, seek and have faith in Him.

When offended, men and women should be easily appeased, slow to anger, and as soon as those who have sinned ask for pardon, the offended party should forgive the sinner with all his or her heart. Even if deep and serious injury has been done to him or her, he or she should not be vengeful, nor bear a brother or sister a grudge in his or her heart.

Abraham, Isaac, and Israel were among the great spirits who were chosen for the roles they were to play in the earth before they were born in the flesh. The Lord also chose the time, place and lineage of these three and named each of them.

The Lord's commands to walk uprightly before Him and become perfect, given to Abraham, Isaac, Israel and their posterity — and to all the world — are part of a test to qualify each soul for eternal life. The covenants He made with Abraham, Isaac and Israel are consonant with His purposes.

Abraham, Isaac, and Israel were among the elect of God and received revelations from Him. They received the priesthood, or power to act for Him and used it to bless the lives of others. They loved the Lord with all their hearts and souls, offered sacrifices, as commanded, and had no other gods before Him. They honored their fathers and mothers. In summary, it has been written of them that they kept the covenants they made with the Lord and passed all of the tests that were put to them. For their efforts and accomplishments they have been granted their exaltation and sit upon their respective celestial thrones.

Abraham, Isaac and Israel each had conferred upon them three great blessings: the rights of the priesthood, kings and birth, sometimes referred to as the crowns of priesthood, kings and gospel (Torah). With these three great blessings men are permitted to act for God, not to achieve their vain ambitions, or to gratify their personal pride, or to control or compel the souls of the children of men in any degree of unrighteousness. Rather, those who hold these powers are to let personal righteousness be the guiding principle in handling and controlling them. (D&C 121:34-46).

Failure to let personal righteousness be the guiding principle in his life caused Reuben, Israel's first born son and natural heir to these three blessings, to forfeit them. Joseph, first born of Israel's second wife Rachel, by contrast, proved to the Lord's satisfaction that personal righteousness was the guiding principle in his life as we shall see as the story unfolds. Joseph fell heir to the birthright blessings. The right of priesthood was conferred upon Levi, and the right of kings was given to Judah.

The life stories of Abraham, Isaac, and Jacob (Israel) and their relationship to Jehovah are reported in another work entitled, *Abraham, Isaac, and Jacob, Servants and Prophets of God.*

More about the lives of the twelve sons of Israel is contained in the chapters that follow beginning with a review of Israel's life, his marriages, the birth of his children and their life in Haran. They are traced to Canaan, the land of promise, and on into Egypt where Levi is the last of them to die about 140 years later.

The lives of the twelve sons were so intertwined with the life of Israel, a reiteration of some previously published material was believed necessary. Chapters I, IX, XII, XIV, XV, XVI and XVII of THE TWELVE SONS of ISRAEL are close copies of Chapters XXI, XXIV, XXV, XXVI, XXVII, and XXVIII of ABRAHAM, ISAAC, AND JACOB, SERVANTS AND PROPHETS OF GOD. This reiteration is for readers who do not have access to the earlier compilation.

Any attempt to reconstruct the life histories of people who lived 3,500 to 3,700 years ago is open to challenge. There are few, if any, original source documents extant, and few people capable of reading and translating them if the documents do exist. Other writings with roots in the ancient past, however, shed light on the lives of the twelve sons of Israel, and their relationship to the Lord God. They include the Masoretic Text of the Holy Scriptures and Legends of the Jews, published by the Jewish Publication Society of America, the King James Version of the Bible, the Joseph Smith Translation, the writings of Josephus — an historian of Antiquity, the Book of Jasher, The Old Testament Pseudepigrapha, the Forgotten Books of Eden, and others.

This effort is not intended as an original work. Rather, it is one of compilation, a putting together of materials from other sources. The language of paraphrase is intended to blend with the language used by the original translators written hundreds of years apart.

The limitations inherent in reconstructing the lives of the twelve sons of Israel are duly noted. The risks are assumed by the compiler. He accepts full responsibility for what is written, attributing any truth this book contains to the living God Jehovah (Yahweh). To himself he consigns any error which might have been inadvertently reported. Hopefully and prayerfully such errors are few and far between.

Dr. Norman L. Heap
Concord, California
January, 1988

THE TWELVE SONGS OF ISRAEL

TABLE OF CONTENTS

	PAGE
Dedication	v
Prologue	vii

CHAPTER TITLES

I	AND THE LORD SAID UNTO JACOB, RETURN UNTO THE LAND OF THY FATHERS... AND I WILL BE WITH THEE	1
II	THE SONS OF ISRAEL AND DAUGHTER DINAH ARRIVE IN CANAAN	13
III	PUT AWAY THE STRANGE GODS THAT ARE AMONG YOU, AND BE CLEAN AND CHANGE YOUR GARMENTS	23
IV	HELP US, O GOD... AND ANSWER US, FOR WE TRUST IN THEE	29
V	THE DEATH OF LEAH, JOSEPH IS SOLD INTO EGYPT	33
VI	AND JOSEPH WAS BROUGHT DOWN TO EGYPT	47
VII	THE MARRIAGES AND FAMILIES OF JOSEPH'S BROTHERS	55

VIII	JOSEPH'S EXPERIENCES IN PRISON	66
IX	ISAAC'S FINAL BLESSINGS, HIS DEATH AND BURIAL	71
X	JOSEPH INTERPRETS THE PHARAOH'S DREAM	74
XI	A MAN DISCREET AND WISE	80
XII	AND THE SEVEN YEARS OF DEARTH BEGAN TO COME, AND JOSEPH'S TEN BRETHREN WENT TO BUY CORN IN EGYPT	87
XIII	O LORD GOD OF HEAVEN AND EARTH, REMEMBER THY COVENANT WITH OUR FATHER ABRAHAM AND DEAL KINDLY WITH MY SONS	95
XIV	AND GOD SENT ME BEFORE YOU TO PRESERVE YOU A POSTERITY IN THE EARTH AND TO SAVE YOUR LIVES BY A GREAT DELIVERANCE	102
XV	AND ISRAEL SAID UNTO JOSEPH, NOW LET ME DIE, SINCE I HAVE SEEN THY FACE, BECAUSE THOU ART YET ALIVE	107
XVI	THOU SHALT CARRY ME OUT OF EGYPT	112
XVII	AND JOSEPH WENT TO BURY HIS FATHER	123
XVIII	FROM THE DEATH OF ISRAEL TO THE DEATH OF LEVI	129
XIX	JOSEPH, SON OF ISRAEL AND RACHEL	132
XX	ZEBULUN, SON OF ISRAEL	144

XXI	SIMEON, SON OF ISRAEL	148
XXII	REUBEN, SON OF ISRAEL	152
XXIII	DAN, SON OF ISRAEL	155
XXIV	ISSACHAR, SON OF ISRAEL	157
XXV	ASHER, SON OF ISRAEL	160
XXVI	GAD, SON OF ISRAEL	162
XXVII	NAPHTALI, SON OF ISRAEL	165
XXVIII	BENJAMIN, SON OF ISRAEL	168
XXIX	JUDAH, SON OF ISRAEL	174
XXX	LEVI, SON OF ISRAEL	178
	EPILOGUE	184

THE TWELVE SONS OF ISRAEL

CHAPTER 1

AND THE LORD SAID UNTO JACOB, RETURN UNTO THE LAND OF THY FATHERS... AND I WILL BE WITH THEE

Jacob, having been robbed by Eliphaz, son of Esau, of all the gifts he planned to give to Laban for a wife, offered, instead, to serve Laban seven years for the younger twin daughter Rachel. Laban agreed saying, "it is better that I give her to thee, than that I should give her to another man: abide with me."[1]

The next seven years of Jacob's life and his feelings about them are reported by Genesis in these words:

"And Jacob served seven years for Rachel; and they seemed unto him but a few days, for the love he had to her."[2]

Jasher reports some other events which took place during those years: the death of Eber at age 464 years in the second year of Jacob's dwelling in Haran (in Jacob's 79th year), and the birth of Reuel, the son of Esau and Basmath, in his third year there. During the fourth year, the first of Laban's three sons, Beor, was born followed by Alib and Chorash. The Lord had blessed Laban on account of Jacob, giving him more sons and daughters. In the fifth year of Jacob's life in Haran, Jehudith, the daughter of Beeri, the wife of Esau died. She left two daughters, Marzith and Puith. After Jehudith died, Esau left Canaan and went hunting in the land of Seir. He took another wife, Ahlibamah, the daughter of Zibeon, the Hivite and brought her back to Canaan. It was Ahlibamah who bore Esau three more sons, Yeush, Yaalar, and Korah.

Esau's cattle and goods were now abundant. They were the source of quarrels with the people of Canaan. He took all his cattle, possessions, wives, and children, and moved to the land of Seir where his descendants intermarried with the Horites and the sons of Seir. He gave Marzith to Anah the son of Zibeon and Puith to Azar the son of Bilhan the Horite.[3]

The seven years of service Jacob gave Laban for Rachel's hand, during which he worked in the house and in the field, came to an end.

> (From Genesis) "And Jacob said unto Laban, Give me my wife, for my days are fulfilled, that I may go in unto her. And Laban gathered together all the men of the place, and made a feast."[4]

To which is added:

> (From Jasher) "And in the evening Laban came to the house and afterward Jacob came there with the people of the feast, and Laban extinquished all the lights that were in the house. And Jacob said unto Laban, Wherefore dost thou do this thing unto us? And Laban answered, such is our custom to act in this land."[5]

Back to Genesis:

> "And it came to pass in the evening, that he took Leah his daughter, and brought her to him, and he went in unto her. And Laban gave unto his daughter Leah Zilpah her maid for a handmaid."[6]

Apparently Jacob didn't realize he had been deceived until the next morning. Jasher embellished the account with descriptions of eating and drinking, the playing of timbrels, dancing and the crowd singing out Heleah, Heleah meaning "she is Leah" which Jacob did not understand.[7]

Continuing Genesis:

> "And it came to pass that in the morning, behold, it was Leah: and he said to Laban, What is this thou hast done unto me? did not I serve with thee for Rachel? wherefore then hast thou beguiled me? And

Laban said, It must not be so done in our country, to give the younger before the firstborn. Fulfill her week, and we will give thee this also for the service which thou shalt give serve with me yet seven other years. And Jacob did so, and fulfilled her week: and he gave him Rachel, his daughter to wife also. And Laban gave to Rachel his daughter Bilhah his handmaid to be her maid. And he went in also unto Rachel and he loved also Rachel more than Leah, and served with him yet seven other years."[8]

Jacob married late in life, an old man by todays' standards. When he did marry he took two wives within a week, Leah and Rachel, and two more within the second seven year period he worked for Rachel's hand. Within a seven year period Jacob married four wives and had twelve children, eleven sons and a daughter. His thirteenth child of record, Benjamin, was not born in Haran, but in Canaan.

Leah apparently had four sons about a year apart, Reuben, Simeon, Levi and Judah, and left bearing temporarily. Rachel could not conceive during this period. She gave Bilhah, her handmaid, to Jacob to wife. Leah followed suit and gave Jacob, her maid Zilpah, to Jacob to wife. Bilhah conceived twice giving birth to Dan and Naphtali. Zilpah conceived twice giving birth to Gad and Asher. Leah again conceived thrice more giving birth to Isaachar, Zebulun, and Dinah.

Joseph was the twelfth child of record to be born to Jacob. Rachel had, at last, conceived after seven years of barrenness.

Actually, Jacob only sought one wife, Rachel. He was given three others, Leah by deception of his father-in-law, Bilhah was given to him by Rachel who thought she couldn't have children (just like Sarah gave to Abraham Hagar) and Leah gave to Jacob, Zilpah, because Leah had finished bearing children. (She thought)

The Genesis account reads:

"And when the Lord saw that Leah was hated, he opened her womb: but Rachel was barren. And Leah conceived, and bare a son, and she called his name Reuben: for she said, Surely the Lord hath looked upon my affliction; now therefore my husband will love me. And she conceived again, and bare a son; and said, Because the Lord hath heard that I was hated, he hath therefore given me this son also: and she called his name Simeon. And she conceived again and bare a son; and said, Now this time will my husband be joined unto me, because I have born him three sons, therefore was his name called Levi. And she conceived again, and bare a son: and she said, Now will I praise the Lord therefore she called his name Judah: and left bearing."[9]

The name of Leah's third son, Levi, say the Legends, was given by God Himself, not by his mother.[10]

(From Genesis) "And when Rachel saw that she bare Jacob no children, Rachel envied her sister; and said unto Jacob, Give me children, or else I die. And Jacob's anger was kindled against Rachel: and he said, Am I in God's stead, who hath withheld from thee the fruit of the womb? And she said, Behold my maid Bilhah, go in unto her; and she shall bear upon my knees that I may have children by her. And she gave him Bilhah her handmaid to wife: and Jacob went in unto her. And Bilhah conceived, and bare Jacob a son. And Rachel said, God hath judged me, and hath also heard my voice, and hath given me a son: therefore called she his name Dan. And Bilhah, Rachel's maid conceived again, and bare Jacob a second son. And Rachel said, With great (mighty) wrestlings have I wrestled with my sister, and I have prevailed: and she called his name Naphtali."[11]

"When Leah saw that she had left bearing, she took Zilpah her maid, and gave her (to) Jacob to wife. And Zilpah Leah's maid bare Jacob a son. And Leah said, A troop cometh (fortune is come): and she called his name Gad. And Zilpah Leah's maid bare a second son. And Leah said, Happy am I, for the daughters will call me blessed (happy): and she called his name Asher."

"And Reuben went in the days of wheat harvest, and found mandrakes in the field, and brought them unto his mother Leah. Then Rachel said to Leah, Give me, I pray thee, of thy son's mandrakes. And she said unto her, Is it a small matter that thou has taken my husband? and wouldest thou take away my son's mandrakes also? And Rachel said, Therefore he shall lie with thee tonight for thy son's mandrakes. And Jacob came out of the field in the evening, and Leah went out to meet him, and said, Thou must come in unto me; for surely I have hired thee with thy son's mandrakes. And he lay with her that night. And God hearkened unto Leah, and she conceived, and bare Jacob a fifth son. And Leah said, God hath given me my hire, because I have given my maiden to my husband: and she called his name Issachar. And Leah conceived again, and bare Jacob a sixth son. And Leah said, God hath endued me with good dowry; now will my husband dwell with me, because I have born him six sons: and she called his name Zebulun. And afterwards she bare a daughter, and she called her name Dinah."[12]

That Zilpah and Bilhah were sisters is stated in Jubilees 28:9. They were reportedly the daughters of Rotheus, a brother of Deborah, Rebekah's nurse.[13]

The opinion that the prophet Elijah belonged to the tribe of Gad is widespread.[14]

Rachel prayed for children and beseeched Him that He take away her reproach.

The Legends report that Leah, Zilpah and Bilhah united their prayers with Jacob and Rachel, together they sought to remove the curse of barreness from Rachel.[15]

(From Genesis) "And God remembered Rachel and God hearkened unto her, and opened her womb. And she conceived, and bare a son; And said, God hath taken away my reproach. And she called his name Joseph; and said, The Lord shall add to me another son."[16]

The holy spirit had revealed to Jacob that the house of his newly born son Joseph would work the destruction of Esau, causing Jacob to declare, "Now I need not fear Esau or his legions," so say the Legends.[17]

As previously mentioned Jacob was ninety one years old at Joseph's birth and Rachel was about thirty five. Fourteen years earlier when Rebekah had counseled Jacob to flee from Esau, she said she would send for him, after his brother Esau's fury had turned away.[18]

Rebekah sent her nurse Deborah, the daughter of Uz, and two of Isaac's servants unto Jacob after Joseph was born. She beckoned him to return to his father's house in the land of Canaan. [19]

Jacob implored Laban to send him back to Canaan with his wives and children, since he had completed the second seven year term of service for Laban or fourteen years altogether. Jacob was persuaded to stay. They negotiated his wages again. They were changed again, this time Jacob worked for the spotted and speckled cattle. Jacob stayed with Laban another six years. During this time the two servants of Isaac returned to Canaan but Deborah stayed with Jacob and served as a maid to his wives and twelve children. [20]

The Lord prospered Jacob and his family these six years with an abundance of speckled and spotted cattle and sheep of large size, of beautiful appearance and very productive. The Lord then implored Jacob to return to the land of his fathers in Canaan. Jacob gathered his family together and then left for Canaan.

The Genesis account of this six year period reads:

"And it came to pass, when Rachel had born Joseph, that Jacob said unto Laban, Send me away, that I may go unto mine own place, and to my country. Give me my wives and my children, for whom I have served thee, and let me go: for thou knowest my service which I have done thee. And Laban said unto him, I pray thee, if I have found favour in thine eyes, tarry: for I have learned by experience that the Lord hath blessed me for thy sake. And he said, Appoint me thy wages and I will give it. And he said to him, Thou knowest how I have served thee, and how thy cattle was with me. For it was little which thou hadst before I came, and it is now increased unto a multitude; and the Lord hath blessed thee since my coming: and now when shall I provide for mine own house also?"

"And he said, What shall I give thee? And Jacob said, Thou shalt not give me anything: if thou wilt do this thing for me, I will again feed and keep thy flock. I will pass through all thy flock today, removing from thence all the speckled and spotted cattle, and all the brown cattle among the sheep, and the spotted and speckled among the goats: and of such shall be my hire. So shall my righteousness answer for me in time to come, when it shall come for my hire before thy face: every one that is not speckled and spotted among the goats, and brown among the sheep, that shall be counted stolen with me. And Laban said, Behold, I would it might be according to thy word."[21]

"And he removed that day the he goats, that were ringstraked and spotted, and all the she goats that were speckled and spotted, and every one that had some white in it, and all the brown among the sheep, and gave them into the hand of his sons. And he set three days journey betwixt himself and Jacob: and Jacob fed the rest of Laban's flocks. And Jacob took him rods of green poplar, and of the hazel chestnut tree: and pilled white strakes in them, and made the white appear which was in the rods. And he set the rods which he had pilled before the flocks in the gutters in the watering troughs when the flocks came to drink, that they should conceive when they came to drink."

"And the flocks conceived before the rods, and brought forth cattle ringstraked, speckled and spotted. And Jacob did separate the lambs, and set the faces of the flocks toward the ringstraked, and all the brown in the flock of Laban; and he put his own flocks by themselves, and put them not unto Laban's cattle. And it came to pass, whensoever the stronger cattle did conceive, that Jacob laid the rods before the eyes of the cattle in the gutters, that they might conceive among the rods. But when the cattle were feeble he put them not in; so the feebler were Laban's, and the stronger Jacob's. And the man increased exceedingly, and had much cattle, and maidservants and menservants and camels and asses. And he heard the words of Laban's sons, saying Jacob hath taken away all that was our father's; and of that which was our father's hath he gotten all this glory. And Jacob beheld the countenance of Laban, and, behold, it was not toward him as before."[22]

Jacob's sheep and cattle were highly sought after by the sons of men, who traded maidservants and menservants, and camels and asses for them, thus explaining how Jacob acquired servants and camels and asses as well as sheep and cattle, though he himself had so recently been a servant of Laban.[23]

The Lord commanded Jacob to return to the land of his fathers and kindred. He identified Himself as the God of Bethel where Jacob had anointed the pillar twenty years before. The place was where

Jacob had vowed saying:

(From Genesis) "If God will be with me, and will keep me in this way that I go and will give me bread to eat, and raiment to put on, so that I come again to my father's house in peace; then shall the Lord be my God: And this stone, which I have set for a pillar, shall be God's house: and of all that thou shalt give me I will surely give the tenth unto thee."[24]

Jacob informed Rachel and Leah of the Lord's command. They agreed to go with him and take Bilhah and Zilpah and all twelve children with them; a small sized exodus in itself which included Jacob's 200 drove of cattle. Rachel took with her the images or idols of her father, Laban. Apparently these images were felt to have astrologic value. Rachel was afraid her father would consult them to ascertain where they had gone. These images were described as skulls of firstborn in which candles were placed, and when lighted were worshipped and consulted.[25]

The journey was begun from Padan-aram enroute to Isaac's abode in Canaan by way of Mount Gilead, without informing Laban. He had gone to shear sheep. Laban was later told. He set out and overtook Jacob's family seven days later. Laban was warned by God in a dream to speak neither good nor bad of Jacob thus tempering his wrath.

The Genesis account reads:

"And the Lord said unto Jacob, Return unto the land of thy fathers, and to thy kindred; and I will be with thee. And Jacob sent and called Rachel and Leah to the field unto his flock, and said unto them, I see your father's countenance, that it is not toward me as before; but the God of my father hath been with me. And ye know that with all my power I have served your father. And your father hath deceived me, and changed my wages ten times; but God suffered him not to hurt me."

"If he said thus, The speckled shall by thy wages, then all the cattle bare speckled: and if he said thus, The ringstraked shall be thy hire; then bare all the cattle ringstraked. Thus God hath taken away the cattle of your father, and given them to me. And it came to pass at the time that the cattle conceived, that I lifted up mine eyes, and saw in a dream, and behold, the rams which leaped upon the cattle were ringstraked, speckled and grisled."

"And the angel of God spake unto me in a dream, saying, Jacob, and I said, Here am I. And he said, Lift up now thine eyes, and see, all the rams which leap upon the cattle are ringstraked, speckled, and grisled: for I have seen all that Laban doeth unto thee. I am the God of Bethel, where thou anointest the pillar, and where thou vowedst a vow unto me: now arise, get thee out from this land, and return unto the land of thy kindred."

"And Rachel and Leah answered and said unto him, Is there yet any portion or inheritance for us in our father's house? Are we not counted of him, strangers? for he hath sold us, and hath quite devoured also our money. For all the riches which God hath taken from our father, that is ours, and our children's; now then, whatsoever, God hath said unto thee, do."[26]

After Laban, his brothers and servants had overtaken Jacob and his family, there were words of disagreement, a review of their twenty years together and eventual reconciliation with Laban kissing his daughters and grandchildren goodbye. Jacob and Laban had entered into a covenant with one another marked by a heap of stones as a witness of that covenant; known to Laban as Jegarsahadutha and to Jacob as Galeed.

As a worshipper of idols Laban sought the influence of false gods and of the stars through those idols (skulls of slain firstborn lighted up with candles) to foretell the future and to guide him.

Even though Laban had just experienced a dream in which the Lord God of Jacob had warned him to "Take heed that thou speak not to Jacob either good or bad," Laban called Jacob to task for stealing his images. Instead, Rachel had taken them, and hid them in the camels furniture. She remained seated on her camel to successfully conceal the images from detection. In so doing she spared her own life, for Jacob had already promised that "with whomsoever thou findest thy gods, let him not live." Laban failed to make good his accusation that Jacob had stolen his gods. Jacob was wroth and unloaded twenty years of frustration on Laban.[27]

Jacob's defense of his own actions brought Laban to reconciliation. A covenant between them resulted. Laban asked that Jacob not afflict his daughters and not take any more wives. Laban and Jacob agreed not to pursue one another past a heap of stones. Jacob offered sacrifice, and broke bread with his brethren. Laban left for his home the next morning after kissing his daughters and grandchildren goodbye.[28]

As Jacob and his family continued their journey toward Canaan and his father Isaac, angels of God met him at a place he named Mahanaim. Jacob sent messengers ahead of his party to his brother Esau who was living in the land of Seir, the country of Edom. Jacob apparently sought safe passage of his family, oxen, asses, flocks, menservants and maidservants. The messengers returned shortly with the news that Esau was already coming to meet Jacob and he had 400 men with him.

Jasher and the Legends report that Laban alerted Esau exciting his anger and hatred toward Jacob. Hence Esau put together his band of 400 men.[29]

Fearing Esau was coming to destroy his family and take his possessions Jacob divided them up (his family) into companies to increase the chances part of them would escape Esau's wrath. Jacob then prayed mightily unto the Lord for delivery from the hand of Esau. Upon finishing his prayer Jacob felt impressed to prepare a gift for his brother Esau, a gift of 200 she goats, 20 he goats, 200 asses, and 20 rams, 30 milk camels and colts, 40 kine (cows), 10 bulls, 20 she asses, and 10 foals. The present for Esau having been prepared and placed ahead of his family in the procession, Jacob took Leah, Rachel, Zilpah and Bilhah, his eleven sons and a daughter across the brook Jabbok.

The rest of the evening Jacob wrestled a man until the breaking of the next day. The man he wrestled was reported to have been an angel of God. Jacob's thigh was thrown out of joint in the process, (at 97 years of age). The messenger of God gave Jacob a blessing and changed his name to Israel. The blessing declared Jacob, now named Israel, a prince who has power with God and with men. Apparently Israel saw God face to face while there. Israel named the place Peniel. In memory of the occasion future generations of Israel were not to eat of the sinew which is upon the hollow of the thigh, because it was the hollow of Jacob's thigh that shrank as a result of events of that night.

Jacob/Israel met Esau. His gift was accepted. Israel and his family were allowed safe passage on to Shalem, a city of Shechem in the land of Canaan. Here Jacob and his family bought a parcel of a field, spread his tent, erected an altar, which he called El-elohe-Israel and made his family a home for awhile. Ages of his family as they settled here were Jacob about 97 years and Leah and Rachel about 41 years. The children ranged in age from about 13 to 6 years of age.[30]

The arduous journey just completed saw Jacob/Israel successfully extricate himself from the bondage imposed by his cousin Laban and from the pent up wrath and anger of his brother Esau. Jacob/Israel was able to forgive and make peace with them both with the help of the Lord. At last he was free to settle his family in Canaan as the Lord commanded.

Shem had died in Isaac's 110th year and Jacob's 50th year, leaving Eber as patriarch of the earth, with Isaac the head of the Lord God's covenant people in Canaan. By Isaac's 139th and Jacob's 79th birthdays, Eber had died. Jacob was two years into his service with Laban when Eber died. Unknown to Jacob, the Lord had groomed him twenty years for his future role as prophet and patriarch of the covenant people. Jacob, with a new name, and his house, the house of Israel, arrived in Canaan in Isaac's 159th year. Israel was to replace Isaac as prophet and patriarch of the Lord's covenant people. The covenant people would soon come to be known as the House of Israel.

The next ten years of his life, from age 98 to 108 years of age, were difficult for Jacob/Israel. He dealt with the defiling of his daughter Dinah, and the consequent rage and actions of his sons. He moved his family back to Bethel at the Lord's request, and built an altar there as he had done more than twenty years before as he fled from Esau enroute to Padan-aram. The Lord reiterated the promises He made to Jacob, and his posterity, and reminded him again that his new name under the covenant was Israel.

We now turn our attention to the teen-age sons and daughter of Israel as they arrive in Canaan with their parents. Joseph, who was then about six or seven years of age, was also with them.

---

1. Genesis 29:18-19 KJV, MT, JST
2. Ibid 29:20 KJV, MT, JST
3. Jasher XXX:15-29
4. Genesis 29:21-22 KJV, MT, JST
5. Jasher XXXI:2-3; Legends I:360-61
6. Genesis 29:23-24 KJV, MT, JST
7. Jasher XXXI:6-9; Legends I:360
8. Genesis 29:25-30; Legends I:361
9. Genesis 29:31-35; Legends I:361-63
10. Legends I:363
11. Genesis 30:1-8; Legends I:364-365
12. Ibid 30:9-21; Legends I:365
13. Legends V:295
14. Ibid II:144-145, V:297
15. Legends I:368
16. Genesis 30:22-24; Legends I:368-69
17. Legends I:369
18. Genesis 27:43-45 KJV, MT, JST
19. Jasher XXXI:22-23; Legends I:369
20. Ibid XXXI:29-30
21. Genesis 30:25-34 KJV, MT, JST
22. Genesis 30:35-43, 31:1-2; Legends I:371
23. Jasher XXXI:31-34
24. Genesis 28:20-22 KJV, MT, JST
25. Jasher XXXI:40-44; Legends I:371
26. Genesis 31:3-16 KJV, MT, JST
27. Genesis 31:25-42: Legends I:374
28. Ibid 43-55: Legends I:374-75
29. Genesis 32:9-12; Legends I:381; Jasher XXXII:16-23
30. Genesis 32:9-32, 33:1-17; Jasher XXXI:16-73; Legends I:381-395

CHAPTER II

THE SONS OF ISRAEL AND DAUGHTER DINAH ARRIVE IN CANAAN

Genesis doesn't say how long it took for Israel to move his family from Haran to Canaan or whether they stopped along the way. We do know that they encountered Esau, and that Israel intended to take his time because of his young family and all the animals. His animals undoubtedly were giving birth along the way. After Esau's departure, the next entry in Genesis tells of Israel's building a house and making booths for his cattle in a place called Succoth.

Jasher and the Legends reported that after leaving the presence of Esau, Israel moved on to the extremity of the land of Canaan in its borders, and remained there some time.[31] Later he moved his family into Canaan where he built booths (corrals) for his cattle. Subsequently, he pitched his tent before, or in front of the city of Shechem. He arranged to buy a parcel of a field where he pitched his tents. The purchase was made from the children of Hamor, Shechem's father, for a hundred pieces of money (Genesis) or five shekals (Jasher).

The Genesis account reads:

"And Jacob journeyed to Succoth, and built him an house, and made booths for his cattle: therefore the name of the place is called Succoth. And Jacob came (in peace) to Shalem, a city of Shechem, which is in the land of Canaan, when he came from Padan-aram, and pitched his tent (encamped) before the city. And he bought a parcel of a field, where he had spread his tent, at the hand of the children of Hamor, Shechem's father, for a hundred pieces of money. And he erected an altar and called it El-elohe-Israel."[32]

Jasher indicated Israel stayed in Succoth a year and six months. He was 99 years old when the Lord appeared and said unto him "Arise and go up to Bethel and remain there," and 100 years old when God reminded him Israel was his name and that he was no more to be called Jacob.[33]

Three years had transpired between Israel's departure from Haran and this command of God for him to be addressed as Israel from now on.

These were difficult years for Israel. His daughter Dinah was ravaged, and the anger of his sons raged out of control. The sons of the city of Shechem were slain by Simeon and Levi. Israel criticized them for overreacting and incurring the wrath of the Canaanites. He had to move his family elsewhere. Elsewhere, the Lord revealed, was Bethel.

Dinah's tragic experience and the reaction of her brothers, followed:

(From Genesis) "And Dinah the daughter of Leah, which she bare unto Jacob, (whom she had borne unto Jacob), went out to see the daughters of the land. And when Shechem the son of Hamor the Hivite, prince of the land (country) saw her he took her and lay with her, and defiled (humbled) her. And his soul clave (did cleave) unto Dinah the daughter of Jacob, and he loved the damsel, and spake kindly (spoke comfortingly) unto the damsel. And Shechem spake unto his father Hamor, saying, Get me this damsel to wife. And Jacob heard that he had defiled Dinah his daughter: now his sons were with his cattle in the field: and Jacob held his peace until they were come."[34]

Jasher and the Legends indicate that there was a celebration going on in the city of Shechem with dancing, and rejoicing among the large crowd of people there. Rachel, Leah and Dinah and their maidservants went to see the daughters of the city and all the great people who were there. Shechem was watching the daughters of the land dance and rejoice. He saw Dinah sitting with her mother Leah. They were also watching the celebration. Shechem was attracted to Dinah and asked his friends who she was.

They told him that she was the daughter of Jacob, the son of Isaac, the Hebrew, and that she had come with her mother and maidservants to watch the celebration. Shechem's soul became fixed upon Dinah. He sent and had her taken by force. Dinah was brought to the house of Shechem where he seized, forcibly raped her, and kept her captive in his house.[35]

They (Leah, Rachel, and their maids) told Israel. He reacted by sending twelve of his servants to retrieve her. His sons were in the field with the cattle. His servants were not successful in freeing Dinah. They were turned away by Shechem and his men. However, they did see Shechem sitting with Dinah, embracing and kissing her before their eyes.

When Israel was told of the failed attempt to retrieve Dinah, he sent two maidens from his servants daughters to take care of her where she was being held captive. He otherwise held his peace while waiting for his teenage sons to come home from their cattle.

In the meantime, Shechem conferred with his father Hamor and requested that he (Hamor) arrange for Dinah to be his (Shechem's) wife. Hamor queried his son saying, "Is there no woman amongst the daughters of thy people that thou wilt take an Hebrew woman who is not of thy people?" "Her only must thou get for me," Shechem replied. Hamor complied.[36]

> (From Genesis) "And Hamor the father of Shechem went out unto Jacob to commune (speak) with him."[37]

The news spread to the sons of Israel. They were fired with anger as they spoke to Father Israel about it saying:

> (From Jasher) "Surely death is due to this man and to his household, because the Lord God of the whole earth commanded Noah and his children that man shall never rob, nor commit adultery; now behold Shechem has both ravaged and committed fornication with our sister, and not one of all the people of the city spoke a word to him. Surely thou knowest and understandest that the judgement of death is due to Shechem, and to his father, and to the whole city on account of the thing which he has done."[38]

(From Genesis) "And the sons of Jacob came out of the field when they heard it: and the men were grieved, and they were very wroth, because he had wrought folly (a vile deed) in Israel in lying with Jacob's daughter; which thing ought not to be done."[39]

Hamor arrived for discussion while the sons of Israel were talking among themselves.

(From Genesis) "And Hamor communed (spoke) with them, saying, The soul of my son Shechem longeth for your daughter: I pray you give her him to wife. And make ye marriages with us, and give your daughters unto us, and take our daughters unto you. And ye shall dwell with us: and the land shall be before you; dwell and trade ye therein, and get you possessions therein."[40]

After Hamor finished speaking with Israel and his sons, Shechem spoke for himself saying, in effect, he would give anything to have Dinah. The sons of Israel (Simeon and Levi) set a condition for the marriage: circumcision of Shechem and Hamor and all the males of their households.

(From Genesis) "And Shechem said unto her father and unto her brethren, Let me find grace (favour) in your eyes, and what ye shall say unto me I will give. Ask me never so much dowry and gift, and I will give according as ye shall say unto me: but give me the damsel to wife."

"And the sons of Jacob answered Shechem and Hamor his father deceitfully (with guile) and said, because he had defiled Dinah their sister: And they said unto them, We cannot do this thing, to give our sister to one that is uncircumcised; for that were a reproach unto us: But in this (only on this condition) will we consent unto you: If ye will be as we be, (are) that every male of you be circumcised; Then will we give our daughters unto you, and we will take your daughters to us, and we will dwell with you, and we will become one people."

"But if ye will not hearken unto us, to be circumcised then (will we take our daughters) we will be gone. And their words pleased Hamor, and Shechem, Hamor's son. And the young man deferred not to do the thing, because he had delight in Jacob's daughter, and he was more honorable than all the house of his father."[41]

The sons of Jacob had bought some time to decide what to do. Pretending they needed to consult with Isaac concerning the matter, they asked Hamor and Shechem to return for an answer in a day or two.[42]

> (From Jasher) "And when they had gone, the sons of Jacob said unto their father, saying, Behold, we know death is due to these wicked ones and to their city, because they transgressed that which God had commanded unto Noah and his children and his seed after them. And also because Shechem did this thing to our sister Dinah in defiling her, for such vileness shall never be done amongst us..."[43]

Simeon goes on to suggest that Shechem, Hamor and all the males of their households be circumcised and when they were "sunk down with pain" they would attack and kill them. The plan was agreed to when Shechem and Hamor came back the next day. The sons of Israel gave them their answer: i.e. you can have Dinah if you will all be circumcised. We then will intermarry with you.[44]

> (From Genesis) "And Hamor and Shechem his son came unto the gate of their city, and communed with the men of their city saying, These men are peaceable with us; therefore let them dwell in the land, and trade therein; for the land behold, it is large enough for them; let us take their daughters to us for wives, and let us give them our daughters."
>
> "Only herein will the men consent unto us for to dwell with us, to be one people, if every male among us be circumcised, as they are circumcised. Shall not their cattle and their substance and every beast of theirs be ours? Only let us consent unto them, and they will dwell with us. And unto Hamor and unto Shechem his son hearkened all that went out of the gate of his city; and every male was circumcised, all that went out of the gate of the city.[45]

Jasher and the Legends report that Shechem and Hamor were held in great esteem by the people of the city and that the men of the city agreed to be circumcised out of respect for them. The men of the city were assembled and the sons of Jacob were called to come and circumcise them. Altogether some six hundred forty five men and two hundred forty six boys were circumcised over a two day period, including Hamor, Shechem, and his five brothers.[46]

Not all of the males were circumcised however. Some reportedly refused including Chiddekem, son of Pered, the father of Hamor, and his six brothers. They wouldn't listen to Hamor. Instead, they became angry with him and refused to be circumcised. It was also discovered that eight small boys had been kept from circumcision by their mothers who apparently had not heard Hamor and Shechem's appeal. The boys were summoned to be circumcised. Chiddekem, the father of Hamor and his six brothers intervened with swords and sought to slay Hamor, his son, Shechem, his grandson, and Dinah as well.

During this confrontation with Chiddekem and his men Shechem and Hamor were asked whether there were no women among the daughters of Canaan that could be taken for wives instead of the daughters of the Hebrews? Chiddekem and his men would hear no more talk of circumcision and, in their eyes, saw no other solution than to slay Hamor and Shechem in addition to all Israel. To save their lives Shechem and Hamor declared that their intentions, all along, were to take Dinah and eventually destroy all Israel and seize their cattle and animals after the pain of their flesh was over.[47]

Dinah, held in Shechem's house, heard some of these conversations Chiddekem and his brothers had had with Hamor and Shechem. She managed to send one of her two maidens to her father Israel with word that Hamor, Shechem, Chiddekem, and all their men would soon fall upon him and his house to destroy them. The message angered the sons of Israel.

(From Jasher) "And Simeon and Levi swore and said, As the Lord liveth, the God of the whole earth, by this time tomorrow, there shall not be a remnant left in the whole city."[48]

(From Genesis) "And it came to pass on the third day, when they were sore, that two of the sons of Jacob, Simeon and Levi, Dinah's brethren, took each man his sword, and came upon the city boldly (unawares) and slew all the males. And they slew Hamor and Shechem his son with the edge of the sword, and took Dinah out of Shechem's house, and went out. The sons of Jacob came upon the slain, and spoiled the city, because they had defiled their sister. They took their sheep, and their oxen and their asses, and that which was in the city, and that which was in the field, and all their wealth, and all their little ones, and their wives took they captive, and spoiled even all that was in the house."[49]

Apparently Simeon and Levi first encountered a body of twenty young men who had not been circumcised, killing eighteen of them. Two escaped. All the rest of the men and many women of the city were reported to have been slain. Some of the women and the children were taken captive. These captives and the spoils of the city, including sheep, oxen and cattle were brought before Israel by Simeon and Levi.[50]

(From Genesis) "And Jacob said to Simeon and Levi, Ye have troubled me to make me to stink (odious) among the inhabitants of the land, among the Canaanites, and the Perizzites: and I being few in number, they shall gather themselves together against me, and slay (smite) me; and I shall be destroyed, I and my house. And they said, should he deal with our sister as with an harlot?"[51]

Israel was concerned that the endless numbers of the Canaanites would overwhelm the relatively small number of his family and servants. He wanted peace with them. Instead, Simeon's and Levi's actions, in effect, picked a fight which Israel wasn't ready for.

In defense of their actions, Simeon and Levi reminded their father that Dinah's chastity had been violated. They called him to task for not speaking out against Shechem's actions. "Shall he deal with our sister as with a harlot in the streets?"[52]

The next entry in Genesis beginning with Chapter 35 reports the move of Jacob/Israel and his family to Bethel at the request of the Lord. Other writings report the experiences of the sons of Israel before going to Bethel including Simeon's marriage to Bunah, one of the Canaanites among those they had taken captive. They also had skirmishes with a Canaanite group.

With the Lord's help they were able to keep from getting into full scale battles with them. The Lord's help was obtained by way of mighty prayers offered by Isaac and Israel. They pleaded for protection and assistance. The answers came by way of the Canaanite kings advisors. The hearts of the kings' advisors were filled with great fear and terror. That fear and terror was communicated to the Canaanite kings. They reviewed Abraham's experiences with Nimrod, with the five kings of Elam with Isaac and they reviewed Jacob's experience with Esau. They were also impressed by Simeon's and Levi's most recent experience in slaughtering the males of Shechem's city.

In other words, when you fight with Israel you come to war with Israel's God. The kings were persuaded not to fight with Israel and his sons at that time.

To be more specific, the two men who escaped from Shechem went to Tapnach whose king was Jashub. They reported what happened. Jashub wondered how two men could do all they claimed. He sent for his advisors. Initially they counselled Jashub to ask seven kings of the Amorites to join his men in a battle intended to destroy Israel and his sons.

As thousands of these warriors assembled and prepared for battle with swords, Israel became aware of them. He complained of Simeon's and Levi's behavior once again. This time Judah answered his father saying:

(From Jasher) "Was it for naught my brothers Simeon and Levi killed all the inhabitants of Shechem? Surely it was because Shechem had humbled our sister, and transgressed the command of our God to Noah and his children, for Shechem took our sister away by force and committed adultery with her."[53]

Judah reviewed the history of the more recent events and encouraged father Israel to have faith in the God who delivered the city of Shechem to them. He also expressed his belief this same God would deliver them from the Canaanite kings. Judah calmed his father with these words: "Now be tranquil about them and cast away thy fear, but trust in the Lord our God, and pray unto him to assist us and deliver us, and we will do unto them as my brothers did unto Shechem."[54]

Assuming the leadership of Israel's sons, Judah counselled them to "Strengthen yourselves and be sons of valor, for the Lord our God is with us, do not fear them." The sons of Israel, their servants and the servants of Isaac, 112 of them altogether, put on their weapons of war to battle the Canaanite thousands.

They also sought help from the mighty God of Isaac even Jehovah through prayer. They pled with Isaac to serve as voice in their behalf. With characteristic faith Isaac complied. His prayer:

> (From Jasher) "O Lord God, thou didst promise my father, saying, I will multiply thy seed as the stars of heaven, and thou didst also promise me, and establish thou thy word, now that the kings of Canaan are coming together, to make war with my children because they committed no violence. Now therefore O Lord God, God of the whole earth, pervert, I pray thee the counsel of these kings that they may not fight against my sons. And impress the hearts of these kings and their people with the terror of my sons....And with thy strong hand and outstretched arm deliver my sons and their servants from them, for power and might are in thy hands to do all this."[55]

With courage, confidence and trust in their God the sons of Israel and their servants went toward the Canaanites. Israel also prayed for their deliverance. His prayer in part:

> (From Jasher) "O may my prayer be acceptable before thee that thou mayest turn to me with thy mercies, to impress the hearts of these kings and their people with the terror of my sons, and terrify them and their camps, and with thy great kindness deliver all those that trust in thee, for it is thou who canst bring people under us and reduce nations under our power."[56]

The Lord heard the prayers of Isaac and Israel and answered them. He filled the hearts of the kings' advisors with such great fear and terror that they decided not to fight Israel and his band of 112. The Canaanite kings became convinced that to fight against Israel was also to fight against Israel's God.

> (From Jasher) "For this proceeded from the Lord to them, for he heard the prayers of Isaac and Jacob, for they trusted in Him; and all these kings returned with their camps on that day, each to his own city, and

they did not at that time fight with the sons of Jacob. And the sons of Jacob kept their station that day till evening opposite mount Sihon, and seeing that these kings did not come to fight against them, the sons of Jacob returned home."[57]

---

31. Jasher XXXII:73; Legends I:394
32. Genesis 33:17-20 KJV, MT, JST; Legends I:394
33. Jasher XXXIII:4, XXXVI:1,8; Legends I:395
34. Genesis 34:1-5 KJV, MT, JST
35. Jasher XXXIII:5-11; Legends I:395-6
36. Jasher XXXIII:12-18; Legends I:396-7
37. Genesis 34:6 KJV, MT, JST
38. Jasher XXXIII:21-22; Legends I:397
39. Genesis 34:17 KJV, MT, JST
40. Ibid 34:8-10 KJV, MT, JST
41. Ibid 34:11-19 KJV, MT, JST
42. Jasher XXXIII:29-33: Legends I:397
43. Ibid XXXIII:34-35; Legends I:397
44. Ibid XXXIII:36-46; Legends I:397
45. Genesis 34:20-24 KJV, MT, JST
46. Jasher XXXIII:46-52, XXXIV:1; Legends I:398
47. Ibid XXXIV:2-18; Legends I:398-399
48. Ibid XXXIV:19-23; Legends I:399
49. Genesis 34:25-29 KJV, MT, JST
50. Jasher XXXIV:24-31; Legends I:399
51. Genesis 34:30-31 KJV, MT, JST
52. Jasher XXXIV:32-34; Legends I:399
53. Jasher XXXIV:32-52; Legends I:400-401
54. Ibid XXXIV; 53-56; Legends I:401
55. Ibid XXXIV:65-68; Legends I:401-402
56. Ibid XXXIV:69-70; Legends I:402
57. Ibid XXXV:1-25; Legends I:403

Chapter III

PUT AWAY THE STRANGE GODS THAT ARE AMONG YOU, AND BE CLEAN AND CHANGE YOUR GARMENTS.

Shortly thereafter, Israel moved his family to Bethel at the Lord's request. He was to build an altar there as he had done twenty years before as he fled from Esau enroute to Padanaram. Apparently Israel had offered no sacrifices unto the Lord while in the service of Laban. Laban worshipped images and other false gods.

After the Lord's visit and before his departure from Shechem Israel counselled his household to live righteously, to purify their tents and to put away their strange gods. These strange gods were brought from the house of Laban and were still among them. They were to be put away in preparation for the making of sacrifices to the Lord God Jehovah in Bethel. Israel admonished them to be clean and to change their garments. His household gave up their strange gods including those which were in their hands and the earrings in their ears.

Apparently Israel never knew until then that Rachel had brought some of these images with her and hid them in the camels furniture. Israel had come upon them by accident. He then hid them under the oak in Shechem before they left.[58]

(From Genesis) "And they gave unto Jacob all the strange gods which were in their hand, and all their earrings' which were in their ears; and Jacob hid them under the oak which was by Shechem."

"And they journeyed: And the terror of God was upon the cities that were round about them, and they did not pursue after the sons of Jacob.

So Jacob came to Luz, which is in the land of Canaan, that is, Bethel, he and all the people that were with him. And he built an altar, and called the place El-beth-el: because there God appeared unto him, when he fled from the face of his brother."[59]

At about this time Deborah (Rebecca's nurse on loan to Leah, Rachel, Bilhah and Zilpah) died and was buried by Israel beneath Bethel under an oak.

(From Genesis) "But Deborah Rebekah's nurse died, and she was buried beneath Beth-el under an oak: and the name of it was called Allon-bachuth", the oak of weeping.[60]

Rebecca, wife of Isaac, and mother of Israel, apparently died in Hebron just prior to Israel's arrival. She was buried in the cave of Mach-pelah next to Abraham and Sarah. Israel mourned much for these two great women in his life. Laban, his cousin and nemesis also died. Esau and his family continued to live in Seir during this period.

Rebecca was remarkably faithful to the God of Abraham and Isaac. She had been raised in an idolatrous home, accustomed in her childhood to the incense burned before idols. A beautiful young woman, she chose to accompany Eliezer from Haran to Canaan to marry Isaac, a man she had never before seen. She was soon converted to the living God of Abraham and Isaac.

Living close to the spirit and possessing the gift of prophecy, Rebecca was able to guide the life of her righteous son Jacob, and at the same time, respect the priesthood of her nearly blind husband, Isaac. She had revealed to her at the birth of her twin sons, that Jacob was the anointed son who would dedicate his life to the Lord. She departed neither to the right or to the left in pursuing that course, seeing to it Jacob got the right blessings at the right time. There are at least eight references to Rebecca's gift of prophecy in the Legends of the Jews. She was considered a woman of valor, devoted and true to Isaac.

In contrast to the pomp and ceremony accompanying the death's of Sarah and Abraham, Rebecca's death and burial were quiet and without fanfare. About twenty-five years Isaac's junior, Rebecca died at age 133. Being nearly blind Isaac was unable to make the funeral arrangements. Esau and his idolatrous wives did not believe in the resurrection of the dead, and Jacob (Israel) was unaware of his mother's death. Rebecca was buried at night in the cave of Mach-pelah with little or no ceremony.[61]

The Lord appeared to Jacob, blessed him and reminded him again of his new name. He was now Israel. Introducing Himself as God Almighty, the Lord assured Israel nations shall be of thee and kings shall come out of thy loins, and reassured him he was now in the land of Abraham and Isaac and that Israel would fall heir to it.

(From Genesis) "And God appeared unto Jacob again, when he came out of Padanaram, and blessed him. And God said unto him, Thy name is Jacob: thy name shall not be called any more Jacob, but Israel shall be thy name: and he called his name Israel. And God said unto him, I am God Almighty (El Shaddai): be fruitful and multiply; a nation and a company of nations shall be of thee, and kings shall come out of thy loins; And the land which I gave Abraham and Isaac, to thee I will give it, and to thy seed after thee will I give the land. And God went up from him in the place where he talked with him."[62]

Jacob (Israel) marked the place where God appeared to him by setting up a pillar of stone. He poured a drink offering and oil thereon and called the place where God spoke unto him, Bethel.

(From Genesis) "And Jacob set up a pillar in the place where he talked with him, even a pillar of stone: And he poured a drink offering there on, and he poured oil there on. And Jacob called the name of the place where God spake to him, Beth-el."[63]

RACHEL DIES IN CHILDBIRTH

Continuing their journey toward Hebron, Israel and his family approached Ephrath or Bethlehem. Rachel, expecting her second child, travailed and died in childbirth at age forty five.[64] She died giving birth to Benjamin, the twelfth son of Israel. She was buried near Ephrath and her grave was marked by a pillar.

(From Genesis) "And they journeyed from Beth-el; and there was but a little way to come to Ephrath: and Rachel travailed, and she had hard labour. And it came to pass, when she was in hard labour, that the midwife said unto her, Fear not, thou shalt have this son also. And it came to pass, as her soul was in departing, (for she died) that she called his name Ben-oni (son of my Saviour or distress): but his father called his name Benjamin (son of the right hand) and Rachel died, and was buried in the way to Ephrath, which is Bethlehem. And Jacob set a pillar upon her grave: that is the pillar of Rachel's grave unto this day."65

Rachel's long term barrenness was a great frustration to her. Her sister Leah, also wife of Israel had given birth to seven children and Zilpah and Bilhah had given birth to five children while she tried unsuccessfully to have one child. Rachel's great beauty didn't matter to her. She wanted children. Eventually after uniting her prayers with Israel's, Leah's, Bilhah's and Zilpah's, God answered and Rachel conceived. She bore Joseph, later recognized as the greatest of the twelve sons of Israel.

Rachel gave her life while in child birth with Benjamin some nine years following Joseph's birth. She had foretold the Lord would give her a second son. She prayed often and was a devoted follower of the God of Abraham, Isaac, and Israel. Like Rebecca and Leah she possessed the gift of prophecy and lived a righteous life.

REUBEN LOOSES THE BIRTHRIGHT, KINGLY AND PRIESTHOOD BLESSINGS THROUGH SERIOUS SIN

Other difficulties followed Israel on the heals of Rachel's death. Israel made his camp beyond the tower of Edar as he continued toward Hebron to be near father Isaac. After Rachel's death Israel had pitched his tent in the tent of Rachel's handmaid Bilhah. Reuben apparently was jealous for his mother Leah on account of this. Filled with anger he entered the tent of Bilhah and thence removed his father's bed.66

(From Genesis) And it came to pass, when Israel dwelt in that land (near the tower of Edar), that Reuben went and lay with Bilhah his father's concubine and Israel heard it."67

The Testament of Reuben reports that Israel had gone ahead to see Isaac in Hebron, while his camp and that of his families were in Edar, near to Ephrath in Bethlehem. While Israel was away Reuben had seen Bilhah bathing. His passions were aroused. He later entered her tent in which father Israel had placed his. There he saw Bilhah drunk and uncovered (naked) in her chamber. Reuben lay with her. She apparently was not aware of it.

> (From Testament of Reuben) "And forth with an angel of God revealed to my father concerning my impiety, and he came and mourned over me, and touched her no more."[68]

After this serious transgression Reuben's remorse lasted seven months during which time he was "sick unto death". He repented over a period of seven years. He had difficulty looking in the face of his father Israel the rest of his life. Israel prayed for Reuben that the anger of God might pass from them. On guard lest he fall into this kind of sin again, Reuben was successful in keeping from it the rest of his life.[69]

Never the less Reuben forfeited the blessings ordinarily belonging to the firstborn, i.e. the rights of birth, kings and priesthood. First Chronicles reports Reuben's loss of the rights of birth and kings in these words:

> "Now the sons of Reuben the firstborn of Israel (for he was the firstborn; but for as much as he defiled his father's bed, his birthright was given unto the sons of Joseph the son of Israel: and the genealogy is not to be reckoned after the birthright, For Judah prevailed above his brethren and of him came the Chief ruler; but the birthright was Joseph's.)"[70]

Apparently, the genealogy of Israel was reckoned not by birthright thereafter, but through the right of Kings given to Judah, through whose lineage the Messiah, was to come.

Jasher elaborates:

> "At that time the portion of the birthright, together with the kingly and priestly offices was removed from the sons of Reuben, for he had profaned his father's bed, and the birthright was given unto Joseph, the kingly office to Judah and the priesthood unto Levi because Reuben had defiled his father's bed."[71]

Had he not sinned this great sin, Reuben may well have had the wonderful experiences which fell to Joseph, Judah and Levi, experiences which are reviewed in the following pages. However Reuben redeemed himself through repentance as we shall see.

Israel moved his family from the tower of Edar on to Hebron.

(From Jasher) "And Jacob and his sons and all belonging to him journeyed and came to Mamre, which is Kireath-arba, that is in Hebron, where Abraham and Isaac sojourned, and Jacob with his sons and all belonging to him, dwelt with his father in Hebron. And his brother Esau and his sons, and all belonging to him went to the land of Seir and dwelt there, and had possessions in the land of Seir, and the children of Esau were fruitful and multiplied exceedingly in the land of Seir."[72]

---

58. Genesis 35:1-5 KJV, MT, JST, Antiquities Book I; XXI:2
59. Ibid 35:5-7 KJV, MT, JST
60. Ibid 35:8 KJV, MT, JST; Jasher XXXVI:3-4; Legends I:413
61. Legends I:415, V:271; Jasher XXXVI:5-7
62. Genesis 35:9-13 KJV, MT, JST
63. Ibid 35:14-15
64. Jasher XXXVI:9-11; Legends I:415 (age 36)
65. Genesis 35:16-20 KJV, MT, JST
66. Jasher XXXVI:13-14; Legends I:415
67. Genesis 35:22 KJV, MT, JST
68. Testament of Reuben I:41 Forgotten Books of Eden
69. Ibid II:1-5
70. 1st Chronicles 5:1-2 KJV,MT,JST
71. Jasher XXXVI:15
72. Ibid XXXVI:19-20

CHAPTER IV

HELP US, O GOD, ...AND ANSWER US FOR WE TRUST IN THEE

Israel and his family lived near his father Isaac for about four years, returning for a time back to Shechem where there was better pasture for his many animals. They dwelt again in that part of a field purchased from Hamor the father of Shechem before Simeon and Levi had smitten the city. The kings of the Canaanites were understandably nervous about Israel's return to Shechem. They prepared to do battle with Israel, his family, and servants.

An elaboration of the experiences of the ten sons of Israel before Joseph's being sold into Egypt follows:

Israel's 105th and Isaac's 165th year was the year Israel and his sons returned to Shechem to the parcel of land they had previously purchased. When the kings of Canaan heard of Israel's return to Shechem they consulted with one another, asking what shall we do about it. Jashub, king of Tapnach, sent word to Elan, king of Gaash, Thuri, king of Shiloh, Parathou, king of Chazar, Susi, king of Sarton, Laban, king of Beth-horna, and Shabir, king of Othnaymah, requesting that they assist him in smiting Jacob the hebrew, his sons and all belonging to him.

These kings assembled with their camps of warriors, thousands of them. When they were ready they sent a challenge to Jacob demanding they have an opportunity to avenge the death of those whom Simeon and Levi had previously slain.

When the ten sons of Israel heard the challenge their anger was kindled. They rose up and put on their weapons of war along with all their servants. The one hundred and twelve warriors of Israel equipped in battle array, moved forward toward the Canaanite legions of warriors, and ascended the heap (hill) of Shechem.

Israel's men were confident of success in battle though badly out numbered, because Israel had offered a mighty prayer and the Lord God Jehovah had answered it. The earth shook, the sun darkened, and the Canaanites came unglued.

Israel's prayer and the Lord's answer as reported by Jasher and the Legends:

"And Jacob prayed to the Lord for his sons, and he spread forth his hands to the Lord, and he said, O God, thou art an Almighty God, thou art our father, thou didst form us and we are the works of thine hands; I pray thee deliver my sons through thy mercy from the hand of their enemies, who are this day coming to fight with them, and save them from their hand, for in thy hand is power and might, to save the few from the many."

"And give unto my sons, thy servants, strength of heart and might to fight with their enemies, to subdue them, and make their enemies fall before them, and let not my sons and their servants die through the hands of the children of Canaan. But if it seemeth good in thine eyes to take away the lives of my sons and their servants, take them in thy great mercy through the hands of thy ministers (angels) that they may not perish this day by the hands of the kings of the Amorites."[73]

The Lord's answer to Israel's prayer was powerful and real. The earth shook from its place and the sun darkened, terrifying the Canaanite kings. They were in awe of the sons of Israel. The sound of chariots, the voices of mighty horses, and the voices of a great army accompanying them were heard. Although composed of only one hundred twelve men Israel's army was made to sound like thousands as they went forth with tremendous shouting advancing toward the Canaanites.

The Canaanites wanted to retreat but were ashamed to do so since they had been beaten so badly several years before by just two of Israel's sons. The armies advanced toward each other. As they did so, the sons of Israel offered their own prayer as follows:

> (From Jasher) "Help us O Lord, help us and answer us, for we trust in thee, and let us not die by the hands of these uncircumcised men who this day have come against us."[74]

Judah led the sons of Israel into battle. He encountered Jashub, king of Tapnach, who was covered with iron and brass from head to foot. After an initial skirmish Judah picked up a stone of sixty sheckels weight, threw it at Jashub and knocked him off his horse. Fighting Jashub in hand to hand combat with swords, Judah smote Jashub at the ankles and cut off his feet. He then severed Jashub's head and cast it next to his feet.

Judah's leadership, strength and courage inspired his men to follow suit. Levi and his twelve servants took on Elan, king of Gaash and his fourteen captains, and slew them with the edge of the sword.[75]

Israel himself slew Thuri, king of Shiloh, Parathai, and Shabir, king of Machmaynah with his bow and arrows. Reportedly only three of Israel's warriors died in these battles that temporarily subsided, only to be resumed again. This time Naphtali and Dan demonstrated their skill and strength in battle alongside Judah, Simeon and Levi. In other battles Gad, Asher, Reuben, Issachar and Zebulun are cited for their contributions in winning the fight. Zebulun was described as a young lad of short stature.

The sons of Israel knew that the strength they were able to exert during these battles had come from the Lord, and they acknowledged the source of their strength and power through prayers of thanksgiving to Him.

The spoil of each of the cities taken by the Sons of Israel when pooled together was immense. These spoils were returned to the Canaanites upon completion of a peace treaty between the Israelites and the Canaanites.

An initiative for peace had begun while they were fighting which eventually resulted in a treaty between Israel's sons and the twentyone kings of Canaan. The agreement was made near Mount Hebron.

Presents were offered the sons of Israel. They were implored to return all the spoils captured from the seven cities of the Amorites. The sons of Israel did so and also returned to the Canaanites the women and children that had been captured.

Peace came between the sons of Israel and the kings of the Canaanites from that day until the Israelites returned from Egypt to inherit the land of Canaan hundreds of years later.[76]

---

73. Ibid XXXVII:14-16; Legends I:400-407
74. Ibid XXXVII:24
75. Ibid XXXVII:25-50; Legends I:408-409
76. Jasher XXXVIII:1-52, XXXIX:1-65, XIL:1-52

CHAPTER V

THE DEATH OF LEAH, JOSEPH IS SOLD INTO EGYPT

After peace was made with the Canaanite kings the sons of Israel journeyed from Shechem to Hebron and dwelt by their grandfather Isaac. They left their flocks and herds in Shechem where there was better pasture. Presumably, Israel's servants were left behind to take care of them. Periodically his sons were sent back to Shechem to look after the welfare of their servants and animals.

Genesis makes no reference to the death of Leah. Jasher and the Legends record that she died at age fifty-one in Hebron in Israel's 106th year or the tenth year after returning to Canaan from Padanaram. Israel with the help of his sons buried her in the cave of Machpelah alongside Abraham, Sarah and Rebekah.[77]

Rachel was also dead. She had been buried near Ephrath or Bethlehem. Zilpah and Bilhah presumably continued to live as part of Israel's family. Like Sarah, Rebekah and Rachel, Leah possessed the gift of prophesy. Through her son Levi the priesthood was continued. Through her son Judah was to come the King of Kings and Lord of Lords, the Son of God even Messiah who would save the world from the sins of its people.

After listing the genealogy of Esau's family in Seir or Edom, Genesis moves on to events which took place when Joseph was about seventeen years of age and Israel was about 108 years of age, or some eleven years after they had left Padanaram.

The fame of Israel's ten older sons had spread throughout the land. With the Lord's help they had defeated the armies of the Canaanite kings. Joseph did not take part in these battles. He and

Benjamin were protected from them. When peace was made Israel and his sons moved from Shechem to Hebron leaving behind in Shechem and environs flocks and herds and some servants to watch over them.

> The Genesis account reads: "And Jacob dwelt in the land wherein his father was a stranger in the land of Canaan. These are the generations (genealogical lines) of Jacob. Joseph being seventeen years old was feeding the flocks with his brethren; and the lad was with the sons of Bilhah, and with the sons of Zilpah, his father's wives: and Joseph brought unto his father their evil report."
>
> "Now Israel loved Joseph more than all his children, because he was the son of his old age: and he made him a coat of many colors. And when his brethren saw that their father loved him more than all his brethren, they hated him, and could not speak peaceably unto him."[78]

Joseph's older brothers were understandably jealous of him. In their eyes they had saved the family of Israel from destruction at the hand of the Canaanites. They had risked their lives, and had with all their might fought battles which they had won. Joseph had not been involved in them. He had done nothing extra ordinary yet, to win the favor of father Israel. Joseph was obviously Israel's favorite, however. His brother's jealousy was contained until Joseph revealed to them two dreams, dreams in which he was exalted above his brethren, and in the second dream, even above his father and mother.

These dreams and his behavior related thereto proved to be too much for Joseph's brethren. They plotted to kill him, but changed their minds and sold him to merchants enroute to Egypt instead.

Joseph had seen the strength of his brethren and their greatness in battle and he extolled them for it. However, he also extolled himself above his brethren and brought evil reports of them to father Israel. Reportedly Joseph told his father that Gad and Asher were slaying the best of the flocks and eating them against the advice of Reuben and Judah. Gad was angry, feeling the report was not fair. It was true, he said, that he had slain a lamb, but the lamb he had slain had been captured and wounded by a bear. Gad slew the bear. The lamb had been so disabled it couldn't live, so the sons of Bilhah and Zilpah butchered and ate it. Gad found it difficult to forgive Joseph and this failure to forgive Joseph for his inaccurate "evil report" cankered Gad's soul during much of his life.[79]

His brethren hated Joseph for his evil reports of them "and could not speak peaceably unto him."[80]

(From Genesis) "And Joseph dreamed a dream, and he told it his brethren; and they hated him yet more. And he said unto them: Hear I pray you, this dream which I have dreamed: For, behold, we were binding sheaves in the field, and, lo, my sheaf arose, and also stood upright; and, behold, your sheaves stood round about, and made obeisance to my sheaf. And his brethren said to him, Shalt thou indeed reign over us? or shalt thou indeed have dominion over us? And they hated him yet the more for his dreams, and for his words."[81]

And as if this were not enough, Joseph dreamed another dream in which even Israel, his father was to bow down unto him (Joseph).

(Continuing Genesis) "And he dreamed yet another dream, and told it his brethren, and said, Behold, I have dreamed a dream more; and, behold, the sun and the moon and the eleven stars made obeisance to me. And he told it to his father, and to his brethren: and his father rebuked him: and said unto him what is this dream that thou hast dreamed? Shall I and thy mother and thy brethren indeed come to bow down ourselves to thee on the earth? And his brethren envied him, but his father observed the saying."[82]

Jasher and the Legends report that Jacob had blessed Joseph and kissed him after Joseph had related the first dream. After dreaming the second dream Joseph told it to his father in the presence of his brethren:

(From Jasher) "And his father heard the words of Joseph and his dream, and seeing that his brethren hated Joseph on account of this matter, Jacob therefore rebuked Joseph before his brethren on account of this thing, saying, what meaneth this dream which thou hast dreamed, and this magnifying thyself before thy brethren who are older than thou art? Dost thou imagine in thy heart that I and thy mother and thy eleven brethren will come and bow down to thee, that thou speakest these things? And his brethren were jealous of him on account of his words and dreams, and they continued to hate him, and Jacob reserved the dreams in his heart."[83]

Though Rachel, mother of Joseph, was dead the dream indicated she would bow down to him. He could have been referring to his foster mother Bilhah who raised him. Jacob reportedly wrote the dream of Joseph down in a book and was convinced of its truth, but for the sake of peace in the family, rebuked Joseph for telling his dreams.[84]

Joseph had received the birthright blessing which would have ordinarily gone to Reuben, just as his father Jacob (Israel) received the birthright blessing which would ordinarily have gone to his brother Esau. Both Reuben and Esau lost these blessings through transgression of God's laws. The Lord let Rebekah know that Jacob (Israel) was the anointed one whom Esau and his posterity would serve. The Lord also let Jacob (Israel) know through Joseph's dreams that Joseph was the anointed one who was to receive the birthright blessings and to whom his brethren would make obeisance. Instead of any further rebuke, Jacob "observed the saying," and "reserved the dreams in his heart". Not so with Joseph's brethren. They had not caught the significance of the birthright blessing, which was bestowed upon Joseph. They envied him instead. This envy was translated into thoughts of killing Joseph. Eventually they sold him.

The opportunity to get even with Joseph came while his brethren were in Shechem feeding their flocks and cattle. Though living near Isaac in the Hebron area, Joseph's ten older brothers had been sent back to Shechem where they had made booths (corrals) for their cattle to facilitate feeding them. "And his brethren went to feed their father's flock in Shechem."[85]

Apparently the sons of Israel were gone longer than expected. He wondered if they had gotten in a fight with the people of Shechem. He called Joseph before him:

(From Genesis) "And Israel said unto Joseph, Do not thy brethren feed the flock in Shechem? Come, I will send thee unto them. And he said to him, Here am I. And he said to him, Go, I pray thee, see whether it be well with thy brethren, and well with the flocks; and bring me word again. So he sent him out of the vale of Hebron, and he came to Shechem."[86]

Joseph departed for Shechem as requested. Apparently he had difficulty finding his brethren.

(From Genesis) "And a certain man found him, and behold, he was wandering in the field: and the man asked him saying, What seekest thou? And he said, I seek my brethren: tell me, I pray thee, where they feed their flocks. And the man said, They are departed hence; for I heard them say, Let us go to Dothan, And Joseph went after his brethren, and found them in Dothan."[87]

Jasher and the Legends indicate Joseph had missed the road or path where he should have turned to find his brothers in the wilderness (field). While wandering in the road Joseph was met by an angel (man) of the Lord who guided him to is brethren.

(From Jasher) "And an angel of the Lord found him wandering in the road toward the field, and Joseph said unto the angel of the Lord, I seek my brethren; hast thou not heard where they are feeding? And the angel of the Lord said unto Joseph, I saw thy brethren feeding here, and I heard them say they would go to feed in Dothan. And Joseph hearkened to the voice of the angel of the Lord, and he went to his brethren in Dothan and he found them in Dothan, feeding the flock. And Joseph advanced to his brethren, and before he had come nigh unto them they resolved to slay him."[88]

(Back to Genesis) "And when they saw him afar off, even before he came near unto them, they conspired against him to slay him. And they said one to another, Behold this dreamer (master of dreams) cometh. Come now therefore, and let us slay him, and cast him into some pit, and we will say, Some evil beast hath devoured him: and we shall see what will become of his dreams. And Reuben heard it, and he delivered him out of their hands and said, Let us not kill him. And Reuben said unto them, Shed no blood, but cast him into this pit that is in the wilderness, and lay no hand upon him; that he might rid him out of their hands, to deliver him to his father again."[89]

Reportedly Joseph's brothers wanted to get even with him but did not know how to do it. Simeon proposed he be killed. Reuben disagreed, proposing Joseph be cast into the pit instead, presumably to die there. However, Reuben really wanted to retrieve Joseph from the pit later and return him to his father.

Antiquities elaborates Reuben's efforts to prevent his brethren from killing Joseph:

"And they already resolved to kill him, and not let slip the opportunity that lay before them; but when Reuben, the eldest of them, saw them thus disposed, and that they had agreed together to execute their purpose, he tried to restrain them, showing them the heinous enterprise they were going about, and the horrid nature of it; that this action would appear wicked in the sight of God, and impious before men...so he entreated them to have a regard for their own consciences, and wisely to consider what mischief would betide them upon the death of so good a child....that they would also fear God, who was already both a spectator and a witness of the designs they had against their brother; that he would love them if they abstained from this act, and yielded to repentance and amendment; but in case they proceeded to do the fact, all sorts of punishment would overtake them from God for this murder of their brother,....He told them further, that their consciences would be their enemies....that it was not a righteous thing to kill a brother though he had injured them....to forget (his) actions....even in things wherein they might seem to have offended....(rather) to unite together in the care of his preservation, that the cause of killing him make the act itself much worse, while they determined to take him off out of envy at his future prosperity, and equal share of which they would naturally partake while he enjoyed it,....that by murdering him, they made it impossible for God to bestow it (the blessings) upon him" (and them).[90]

When Reuben saw he could not persuade his brethren to return Joseph to their father he sought to have him placed in a pit where Joseph would just die rather than be killed at their hand. Reuben intended and did later come for the purpose of retrieving Joseph from the pit and returning him to father Israel.

(From Antiquities) "He begged of them, therefore, not to kill their brother with their own hands, but to cast him into a pit that was hard by, and so let him die....that they would not defile their own hands with his blood. To which the young men readily agreed; so Reubel took the lad, and tied him to a cord and let him down gently into the pit, for it had not water in it; who when he had done this, went his way to seek for such pasturage as was fit for feeding his flocks."[91]

(From Genesis) "And it came to pass, when Joseph was come unto his brethren, that they stript Joseph out of his coat of many colors that was on him. And they took him and cast him into a pit: And the pit was empty, and had no water in it."[92]

The pit reportedly contained serpents and scorpions. Afraid of them, Joseph cried out with a loud voice unto the Lord. The Lord intervened. The serpents and scorpions did him no harm.

Joseph pled with his brethren calling out from the pit:

(From Jasher) "What have I done unto you, and in what have I sinned? Why do you not fear the Lord concerning me? Am I not of your bones and flesh, and is not Jacob your father, my father?....and he continued to cry out and call unto his brethren from the pit, and he said, O Judah, Simeon, and Levi, my brethren, lift me up from the place of darkness in which you have placed me, and come this day to have compassion on me, ye children of the Lord, and sons of Jacob my father. And if I have sinned unto you, are you not the Sons of Abraham, Isaac, and Jacob? If they saw an orphan they had compassion over him, or one that was hungry, they gave him bread to eat, or one that was thirsty, they gave him water to drink, or one that was naked, they covered him with garments."

"And how then will you withhold your pity from your brother, for I am of your flesh and bones, and if I have sinned unto you, surely you will do this on account of my father! And Joseph spoke these words from the pit, and his brethren would not listen to him....and all his brethren heard his cries and weeping in the pit, and his brethren went and removed themselves from the pit, so that they might not hear the cries of Joseph...."[93]

After removing themselves the distance of a bowshot, far enough so they could not hear Joseph's cries, they sat down to eat bread and decide what they would do with him. Should they slay him, leave him in the pit to die, or take him back to father Israel. While thus engaged, a company of Ishmeelites approached. They were enroute to Egypt carrying spices, balms, and myrrh. Their presence gave rise to new choice in dealing with Joseph. Judah suggested they sell Joseph to the Ishmeelites. His brethren agreed. However, before they could implement the plan, seven Midianite merchant men, also passing by, drew Joseph from the pit and queried him. They had thought the pit might contain water and had approached it for that purpose. They found Joseph in the pit rather than water. They pulled him up out of the pit and brought him along with them.

His brethren intercepted the Midianite merchants, claimed Joseph was a recalcitrant servant they had placed in the pit as a disciplinary measure, and demanded he be released to them. The Midianite merchants were not convinced that Joseph was their servant as claimed. Rather than fight over him, however, they offered to buy Joseph for 20 pieces of silver. The offer was accepted and Joseph's brethren were paid.

Reuben apparently was not with his brethren when the sale took place. He had gone to look for pasture. When he returned to the pit Joseph was not there.

The Jasher and Antiquities accounts continue the story. After having purchased Joseph from his brethren the Midianite merchants began to have second thoughts. Perhaps the youth had been stolen from the land of the Hebrews, perhaps we shall die through him. The Testament of Joseph indicates Joseph kept his peace and did not reveal he was really their brother, rather than a slave, so as not to embarrass them.[94]

As doubts about the wisdom of their purchase dwelled within them they looked and saw the company of Ishmeelites which Joseph's brethren had previously seen, approaching. They decided to get rid of Joseph by selling him to the Ishmeelites for twenty pieces of silver, just what they had paid for him. The transaction was completed and the Ishmeelites continued on their way to Egypt.[95]

As previously mentioned, Reuben's intentions were to retrieve

Joseph and return him to his father. When Reuben found Joseph was not in the pit, he tore his garments. His brothers told Reuben what they had done. They had sold him, killed a kid, spread its blood on Joseph's coat, and pretended the coat had been found in a field. Israel later identified the coat as belonging to Joseph and assumed a wild beast had devoured him.

The Genesis account reads:

> "And they sat down to eat bread: And they lifted up their eyes and looked, and, behold, a company of Ishmeelites came from Gilead with their camels bearing spicery and balm and myrrh, going to carry it down to Egypt. And Judah said unto his brethren, what profit is it if we slay our brother, and conceal his blood? Come, and let us sell him to the Ishmeelites, and let not our hand be upon him: for he is our brother, and our flesh, And his brethren were content. Then there passed by Midianite merchant men, and they drew and lifted up Joseph out of the pit, and sold Joseph to the Ishmeelites for twenty pieces of silver: and they brought Joseph into Egypt."

> "And Reuben returned unto the pit; and Behold, Joseph was not in the pit; and he rent his clothes. And he returned unto his brethren and said, The child is not; and I, whither shall I go? And they took Joseph's coat, and killed a kid of the goats, and dipped the coat in the blood; And they sent the coat of many colours, and they brought it to their father; and said, This have we found: know whether it be thy son's coat or no. And he knew it, and said, It is my son's coat; an evil beast hath devoured him; Joseph is without doubt rent in pieces. And Jacob rent his clothes, and put sack cloth upon his loins, and mourned for his son many days."

> "And all his sons and all his daughters rose up to comfort him; but he refused to be comforted; and he said, For I will go down into the grave unto my son mourning. Thus his father wept for him. And the Midianites sold him into Egypt unto Potiphar, an officer (eunuch, which often designates a royal official) of Pharaoh's, and captain of the guard."[96]

Note that verse twenty eight of Genesis Chapter thirty seven reports that the Midianites had sold Joseph to the Ishmeelites who brought Joseph to Egypt. Verse thirty six of the same chapter reports it was the Midianites who sold Joseph unto Potiphar.

Joseph's experiences enroute to Egypt were reported by Jasher and the Legends.

At first the Ishmaelites let Joseph ride one of their camels. Realizing he was leaving the land of his fathers, Joseph began to weep. The Ishmaelites made him get off the camel and walk. Unable to continue walking on account of the bitterness of his soul, Joseph was therefore beaten and afflicted, as incentive to get up and walk. Their journey took them past Rachel's grave near Ephrath. He fell upon his mother's grave and wept. He cried out and unburdened his soul unto her. Joseph pled for his mother to speak to him from the grave.

At last she responded by saying:

(From Jasher and the Legends) "My son, my son Joseph, I have heard the voice of thy weeping and the voice of thy lamentation; I have seen thy tears; I know thy troubles, my son, and it grieves me for thy sake, and abundant grief is added to my grief. Now therefore my son, Joseph, my son, hope to the Lord, and wait for him, and do not fear, for the Lord is with thee, he will deliver thee from all trouble. Rise my son, go down unto Egypt with thy masters, and do not fear, for the Lord is with thee, my son. And she continued to speak like unto these words unto Joseph and she was still."[97]

Joseph tried to persuade his Ishmeelite masters to take him back to Israel. They would not listen to or believe him. They beat and afflicted him the rest of the journey. For doing so however, the Lord sent darkness to envelope the earth, thunder and lightnings and mighty wind. Their animals froze and were unwilling to move forward even when beaten. The Ishmeelites pondered what Joseph had told them. They began to realize the Lord had sent these storms on account of Joseph. The Ishmeelites sought his forgiveness and Joseph freely forgave them. The storms lifted, the beasts of burden rose up, the earth was tranquilized and the journey proceeded on to Egypt.

The Ishmeelites counseled one with another concerning the events which had just transpired. At first they thought of taking Joseph back to Canaan. Concluding the return journey would take too long they agreed with one another to sell Joseph to the Egyptians instead, for a high price and be rid of him who caused them so much trouble. Thus they did.[98]

From the Testament of Joseph we learn that enroute to Egypt Joseph claimed to be the slave of Israel and the servant of a trader to whom he had been sold. He failed to mention he was actually Israel's son so as not to embarrass his brothers who had sold him.

> "As I was going with the Ishmeelites, they kept asking me, Are you a slave? And I replied, I am a slave out of a household, so as not to disgrace my brothers. The greatest of them said to me, you are not a slave; even your appearance discloses that, But I told them that I was a slave. As we were reaching Egypt they began to squabble over me as to which of them would put up the money and take me. Accordingly it seemed good to all of them that I should be left in Egypt with a trader handling their trading post until they returned bringing their merchandise. The Lord granted me favor in the eyes of the trader and he entrusted me with his household. And God blessed him by my hand, And he prospered in gold and silver and in business. And I was with him three months."

> "At that time the Memphian woman, Pentephres' wife, came down in a palanquin with great splendor, because she had heard about me from one of her eunuchs. She said to her husband that through a certain Hebrew the trader had become rich; they say that he surely stole him out of Canaan. Now then, work justice concerning him; take the young man to your household, and the God of the Hebrews will bless you, because grace from heaven is with you."[99]

Returning now to the story of Joseph's brethren, as they mire themselves deeper in falsehood and bring much grief to their father Israel:

After the sons of Israel had sold brother Joseph to the Midianites they were conscience stricken, so much so that they wanted to undo what they had just done. It was too late. Joseph had been sold by the Midianites to the Ishmeelites almost immediately after acquiring him. As previously mentioned, Reuben was not present when Joseph was sold. He returned to the pit in the nighttime by himself and found Joseph gone. He called out to him and received no answer. He tore his garments and cried out, "the child is not there, and how shall I reconcile my father about him if he be dead?" His conscience stricken brothers confessed to Reuben what they had done. They discussed how to reconcile father Israel to it. Reuben criticized them for what they had done, but was relieved Joseph had not been killed.[100]

A verbal agreement was reached among them that none would tell Israel the truth i.e. That they had sold Joseph, and they did not know for sure where he had been taken. Death by sword would come to anyone of them by all the rest, if the truth were revealed to Israel or any of his family. Having settled the issue that the truth would not be told Israel, they sat down to invent something to tell him.

Isaachar reportedly suggested that Joseph's coat be torn and that blood of a goat kid be smeared on it. He also suggested that the torn coat filled with blood be taken to their father for identification. His suggestions pleased the other sons of Israel. They followed through. They tore Joseph's coat, killed a kid of goat and spilled its blood on it. The coat was then trampled in the dust and given to Naphtali. Naphtali was commanded by his brethren to take the coat to father Israel.

This was the story they made up which Naphtali was to tell Israel.

> (From Jasher) "We gathered in the cattle and had come as far as the road to Shechem and farther, when we found this coat upon the road in the wilderness dipped in blood and in dust; now therefore know whether it be thy son's coat or not. And Naphtali went and he came unto his father and he gave him the coat, and he spoke unto him all the words which his brethren had commanded him. And Jacob saw Joseph's coat and he knew it and he fell upon his face to the ground, and became as still as a stone, and he afterward rose up and cried out with a loud and weeping voice and he said, It is the coat of my son Joseph."[101]

Israel hastened and sent a servant unto his sons. They reached

Israel's tent about evening. Israel asked them to describe how they came upon the coat. Digging themselves in deeper, they lied again telling Israel that they found the coat while gathering in the flock. Thinking it might be Joseph's, they sent the coat ahead with Naphtali to Israel to be sure.

Israel explained to them that Joseph was sent to see if his brothers had run into foul play since they had been gone longer than anticipated. Again Israel's sons lied to him. They claimed Joseph never came to them nor had they seen him. Israel wept bitterly conceding the coat was Joseph's and he must have been devoured by a wild beast. Feelings of guilt enveloped him. He thought it was his fault Joseph had been devoured. Joseph had been on father Israel's errand. Israel continued to lament wishing aloud death had come to himself instead.

His great mourning affected even his sons who were guilty of this great lie. They wept bitterly too, and so did all of Israel's household.

Judah comforted his father holding his head on his lap wiping the tears from his cheeks. Word was taken to Isaac. He and his servants came to Israel to comfort him, but he refused to be comforted. After much mourning Israel sent his sons to find what was left of
Joseph's body to bring it for burial. Obviously they did not find it, for Joseph had been sold instead. Israel mourned for his son Joseph many days.[102]

---

77.   Jasher XLV:1-3
78.   Genesis 37:1-4 KJV, MT, JST (The Septuagent word indicates many colour, but the Hebrew term may indicate simply long coat with sleeves)
79.   Testament of Gad I:1-36; II:1-21 The Forgotten Books of Eden
80.   Genesis 37:4; Jasher XLI:5-8; Legends II:6-9
81.   Ibid 37:5-8 KJV, MT, JST
82.   Ibid 37:9-11 KJV, MT, JST
83.   Jasher XLI: 15-17
84.   Philo, De Josepho 2; Antiquities Book II, I:2-3
85.   Genesis 37:12 KJV, MT, JST; Legends II:9, V Yashar Wa-Yeshel 80b
86.   Ibid 37:13-14 KJV, MT, JST
87.   Ibid 37:15-17 KJV, MT, JST
88.   Jasher XLI:22-24 see also Legends II:10; V Yashar Wa-Yeheb (The angel was Gabriel in human form).

89. Genesis 37:18-22 KJV, MT, JST
90. Antiquities Book II Ch III:1
91. Ibid Book II, Ch III:2
92. Genesis 37:23-24 KJV, MT, JST
93. Jasher XLI: 29-36 see also Legends II:13-14; V. Yashar Wa Yasheb 81a
94. Testament of Joseph Pg 823:15; Pseudepigraphia
95. Jasher XLII, XLIII, see also Legends II:5-17; V. Yashar Wa Yasheb 81b-82a
96. Genesis 37:25-36 KJV, MT, JST
97. Jasher XLII 25:40 see also Legends II:19-21; V. Yashar Wa Yasheb 82b-84l, 85b-86a
98. Ibid XLII:41-53 see also Legends II:21-22; V. Yashar Wa Yasheb 82b-86a
99. Testament of Joseph p 822:11-12 see also Legends II:24; V. Yashar Wa Yasheb-84b-84b
100. Antiquities Book II Ch II 2-3 see also Legends II:24; V. Yashar Wa Yasheb 84a-84b
101. Jasher XLIII:1-16 see also Legends II:25; V. Yashar Wa Yasheb 84l-84b
102. Ibid XLIII:17-48 see also Legends II:25-28; V. Yashar Wa Yasheb 84a-88a

Chapter VI

AND JOSEPH WAS BROUGHT DOWN TO EGYPT....

(From Genesis) "And Joseph was brought down to Egypt, and Potiphar, officer of Pharaoh, captain of the guard, an Egyptian, bought him after the hands of Ishmeelites, which had brought him down thither."[103]

The Ishmeelites had already determined to sell Joseph for a high price to be rid of him, since they believed he was responsible for all the trouble they had had. They actively sought to sell him as soon as they arrived, and reportedly did so to four men of Medan, son of Abraham. They in turn sold Joseph to Potiphar. The Ishmeelites were called upon to verify Joseph was indeed a slave available for purchase. They affirmed Joseph was a slave and so the transaction was completed. Potiphar took Joseph into his house.[104]

(From Genesis) "And the Lord was with Joseph, and he was a prosperous man; and he was in the house of his master the Egyptian. And his master saw that the Lord was with him, and that the Lord made all that he did to prosper in his hand. And Joseph found grace in his sight, and he served him: And he made him overseer over his house, and all that he had he put into his hand."

"And it came to pass from the time he had made him overseer in his house, and over all that he had, that the Lord blessed the Egyptian's house for Joseph's sake; and the blessing of the Lord was upon all that he had in the house, and in the field. And he left all that he had in Joseph's hand; and he knew not ought he had, save the bread which he did eat. And Joseph was a goodly person and well favored (of beautiful form, and fair to look upon)."[105]

Frequently the Lord God prospers those around the anointed one, even if the anointed one is in bondage, or enslaved. He prospered the Pharaoh and King Abimelech on Abraham's account; He prospered King Abimelech, son of Abimelech on Isaac's account; He prospered Laban on Jacob's (Israel's) account; and He prospered Potiphar on account of Joseph. Each of these four, Abraham, Isaac, Israel and Joseph were anointed servants of God with important missions to fulfill in their lives. They worked to achieve God's purposes concerning His covenant people and for all the world. Eternal principles were taught each of them as they overcame adversity and the tribulations of their lives.

Much has been written of the next episode in Joseph's life. Antiquities refers to it as the signal chastity of Joseph. Nearly one half of the Testament of Joseph is devoted to the subject. The Testament of Joseph is reported in the Forgotten Books of Eden, in the Old Testament Psuedepigrapha volume I, and in the Legends of the Jews volume II. Jasher devotes four pages to the subject. The Genesis account reports it in about 13 verses.

It is not known how long it took for Joseph to be moved from Canaan to Egypt, or how long it took for him to gain the confidence of Potiphar.

(From Jasher) "And Joseph was eighteen years old, a youth with beautiful eyes and of comely appearance, and like unto him was not in the whole land of Egypt."[106]

(From Genesis) "And it came to pass after these things, that his master's wife cast her eyes upon Joseph and she said, Lie with me. But he refused, and said unto his master's wife, Behold, my master wotteth not what is with me in the house, and he hath committed all that he hath to my hand; There is none greater in this house than I, neither hath he kept back anything from me but thee, because thou art his wife; how then can I do this great wickedness and sin against God?"....

"And it came to pass about this time, that Joseph went into the house to do his business; and there was none of the men of the house there within. And she caught him by the garment, saying, Lie with me: and he left his garment in her hand and fled and got him out. And it came to pass that he had left his garment in her hand and was fled forth, That she called unto the men of her house, and spake unto them, saying, see, he hath brought in an Hebrew into us to mock us; and he came in unto me to lie with me, and I cried with a loud voice: and it came to pass, when he heard that I lifted up my voice and cried, that he left his garment with me, and fled, and got him out, and she laid up his garment by her, until his lord came home."

"And she spake unto him according to these words, saying, The Hebrew servant, which thou has brought unto us, came in unto me to mock me. And it came to pass, as I lifted up my voice, and cried, that he left his garment with me and fled out, And it came to pass, when his master heard the words of his wife, which she spake unto him, saying, After this manner did thy servant to me, that his wrath was kindled. And Joseph's master took him and put him into the prison, a place where the king's prisoners were bound; and he was there in the prison."[107]

The Testament of Joseph reports that Potiphar's wife had heard of Joseph's great beauty from one of her eunuchs and that she orchestrated Joseph's purchase from the beginning, indicating she wanted to see him "by reason of her sinful passion," of which Joseph was unaware.[108a]

Zelicah (Zuleika) was the name ascribed to the wife of Potiphar by Jasher and the Legends. She coveted Joseph's beauty and lusted after his body. Her soul was fixed on him and she enticed him daily to go to bed with her. She flirted with him continuously and flattered him with high compliment calling him the most beautiful of all the slaves she had ever seen. Joseph responded by saying, "Surely he who created me in my mother's womb created all mankind." She countered, "How beautiful are thine eyes, with which thou hast dazzled all the inhabitants of Egypt, men and women; and he said unto her, How beautiful they are while we are alive, but shouldst thou behold them in the grave, surely thou wouldst move away from them." She praised his words and his voice and spoke of the beauty of his hair. Joseph responded, "How beautiful and pleasing are my words when I speak the praise of God and his glory." In spite of all her efforts she could not get Joseph to look at her, or to lay with her. She threatened him with death or imprisonment if he resisted her further. Joseph answered, "surely God who created man looseth the fetters of prisoners, and it is he who will deliver me from the prison and thy judgement."

Zelicah was so enamored with Joseph, and consumed by her desire for him that she became ill. Her friends queried her and explained that given the position of her husband, she could have anything she wanted. Zelicah put on a banquet to show her friends why she was so taken by Joseph. She commanded her servants to dress Joseph in costly garments and caused that he should appear before the women. The women were mesmerized by his stunning appearance and beauty. They could not take their eyes off him. They even cut themselves as they peeled citrons (oranges) served at the banquet and the blood from their wounds flowed on their garments. They said, "This slave in your house has overcome us, and we could not turn our eyelids from him on account of his beauty."

Zelicah's friends were convinced that Joseph was the most handsome and desired man around. Again they said to her, in your position you should be able to have him. They encouraged her to use all her charms to cause him to surrender to her.[108b]

She continued to plead with Joseph, enticing him at every opportunity, without success.

One day the brook of Egypt (Nile River) overflowed its banks, and, as was the custom on such occasions, the inhabitants of Egypt including kings and princes celebrated with timbrels and dances and rejoicing. A holiday was declared as the sea of Sihor was inundated. The house of Potiphar participated with the rest of Egypt. Zelicah did not go for she was lovesick. Alone in the house she dressed herself in princely garments, put on her jewels, made up her face, perfumed the temple and the house with cassia and frankincense, and she spread myrrh and aloes. When ready she sat in the entrance to await Joseph as he passed by to do his work. He came in from the field. As Joseph saw her at the entrance he turned back. She called to him and said she would let him pass. He did so and went to his work place in the house.

Zelicah approached him in her princely garments and the scent of her garments spread forth. She hastened to Joseph as he started to leave. She caught hold of him by his garments and declared; "As the king liveth, if thou wilt not perform my request, thou shalt die this day, and she hastened and stretched forth her other hand and drew a sword from beneath her garments and she placed it upon Joseph's neck, and she said, Rise and perform my request, and if not thou diest this day."

Joseph sought to flee, but she seized the front of his garments. In flight his garments were torn from him. Zelicah held on to them as Joseph fled from her and from his garments which were left behind.[108c] The Testament of Joseph reports he fled naked from her as she clung to his garments.[108d]

Acting with cunning Zelicah put off the garments in which she was dressed, and replaced them with more conventional ones. She took the clothes torn from Joseph's back, laid them beside her where she sat in her illness, and called for help. A young lad had returned to the house by then. He responded. She ordered him to gather the people of the house together. When they were assembled, she declared that Joseph had tried to seduce her, even to rape her. She resisted his advances, and tore his garments from him as he responded to her screams and fled for fear of his life. The people of the house believed her. Their wrath was very much kindled against Joseph. They quickly informed Potiphar of the words of Zelicah.

Potiphar was enraged. Zelicah reaffirmed to him the lies she had told his servants. Potiphar ordered Joseph to be beaten with severe stripes.

While being beaten Joseph cried out to his God, "O Lord God, thou knowest that I am innocent of all these things, and why shall I die this day through falsehood, by the hand of these uncircumcised wicked men whom thou knowest?"

The Lord God of heaven answered Joseph's prayer through the mouth of an eleven month old child of Potiphar, who spoke these words as the beating continued: "What do you want of this man, and why do you do evil unto him? My mother speaketh falsely and uttereth lies; thus was the transaction. And the child told them accurately all that happened and all the words of Zelicah to Joseph day after day, he declared unto them." With the report finished the child spoke no word as before. The men wondered greatly. Potiphar abashed and ashamed ordered the beating stopped. He brought Joseph before the judges of the land. They questioned him. Joseph declared Zelicah's claims untrue, and swore by the living God that he had not sought to lie with her or do anything like unto it.

They sent for the garment Joseph left behind as he fled the scene of the alledged wrong doing. From the tear in it the judges were convinced the garments were torn as a result of Joseph's efforts to flee from her clutches. They concluded Joseph was not worthy of death. However, they didn't want to set him free from prison because it would embarrass Potiphar and his wife Zelicah. So Joseph was placed in the prison house where he was confined the next twelve years.

Joseph was not free from Zelicah's enticements, even in prison. She visited him often and enticed him to give in to her and she would have him set free. When Joseph explained to her how wrong it would be for him to commit adultery, she offered to kill her husband, marry Joseph and have him take Potiphar's place. Joseph condemned her evil thoughts and pled with the Lord to be free of her enticements.[108e]

Before he was imprisoned Joseph fasted and prayed, sometimes three days in a row, to be free of her. The food saved from his fasting was given to the poor and the ill.[108f] While in prison she visited him and pled with him to perform her request and she would set him free and even elevate him. Joseph answered;

"It is better for me to remain in this (prison) house than to hearken to thy words, to sin against God; and she said unto him, If thou wilt not perform my wish, I will pluck out thine eyes, add fetters to thy feet, and will deliver thee into the hands of them whom thou didst not know before. And Joseph answered her and said, Behold the God of the whole earth is able to deliver me from all that thou canst do unto me, for he openeth the eyes of the blind, and looseth those that are bound, and preserveth all strangers who are unacquainted with the land."[108g]

Zelicah even offered to give up her idols and to convince her husband to do the same if Joseph would only have intercourse with her. Joseph countered saying:

> "The Lord did not want worshippers who came by means of uncleaness, nor would he be pleased with adulterers, but with those who were pure in heart and undefiled in speech. She was consumed with jealousy, wanting to fulfill her desire. But I devoted myself the more to fasting and prayer that the Lord might rescue me from her."[108h]

On another occasion Zelicah threatened to kill her husband by drug and take Joseph as her husband. Joseph pled with her not to do that wicked deed, commanding her to show reverence to God. She also sent him poisoned food, which Joseph discerned by the gift and power of God. He refused to eat it. She threatened to kill herself. Joseph counselled her not to do that. Joseph viewed his imprisonment by Potiphar as an answer to his prayers that he be delivered from Zelicah's grasp. He gave thanks to the Lord and sang praise in the house of darkness (prison). Through her trumped up charge he was set free from her at last. He glorified God with cheerful voice even in prison saying, "God loves more the one who is faithful in self control and purity with patience and prayer with fasting in humility in heart, the Lord will dwell among you, because he loves self control."[108i]

When Zelicah found she could not persuade Joseph to do evil, even to free himself from prison, she left off going there to entice him.

---

103. Genesis 39:1 KJV, MT, JST
104. Jasher XLIV:1-11 see also Legends II 23, 39-44; V Yashar Wa Yesheb 82b-86a
105. Genesis 39:2-6 KJV, MT, JST
106. Jasher XLIV:14
107. Genesis 39:7-20 KJV, MT, JST
108a. Testament of Joseph, The Forgotten Books of Eden p. 262-263; The Old Testament Psuedepigrapha I p. 822-23; Legends II: p. 39-40
108b. Jasher XLIV:15-38 see also Legends II:47-50; V Yashar Wa Yesheb 86b-7a-87b
108c. Jasher XLIV:39-54 see also Legends II:51-55; V Yashar Wa Yesheb 88a
108d. Testament of Joseph, The Old Testament Pseudepigrapha I p. 821; The Forgotten Books of Eden p. 262

108e. Jasher XLIV:55-80 see also Legends II:56-60
108f. Testament of Joseph; The Old Testament Pseudepigrapha I:820; The Forgotten Books of Eden p. 260
108g. Jasher XLIV:55-80 see also Legends II:55-58; V Yashar Wa Yesheb 88a-89a
108h. Testament of Joseph; The Old Testament Pseudepigrapha I p. 820; The Forgotten Books of Eden P. 260
108i. Ibid p. 820, p. 260

CHAPTER VII

THE MARRIAGES AND FAMILIES OF JOSEPH'S BROTHERS

Joseph was separated from his brethren more than twenty-two years. He had been sold into Egypt at age seventeen. His brethren and their families along with father Israel arrived in Egypt settling in Goshen in Joseph's thirty-ninth year. Some of his brethren were likely married and had begun their families before Joseph was sold into Egypt. The rest were subsequently married and had families by the time of the famine of bread which brought them to Egypt. Our attention is now focused on them.

REUBEN, born of Leah and Israel:

(From Genesis) "Reuben, Jacob's first born. And the sons of Reuben; Hanoch, and Phallin, and Hezron, and Carmi." Thus reports Genesis as the family of Reuben at the time the children of Israel went to Egypt to escape the famine.[109]

To which Jasher and the Legends add:

"So Reuben the son of Jacob went to Timnah and took for a wife Eluiram, the daughter of Avi (Uzzi) the Canaanite and he came to her. And Eluiran the wife of Reuben conceived and bare him Hanoch, Paln, Chetzron, and Carmi, four sons."[110]

SIMEON, born of Leah & Israel:

(From Genesis) "And the sons of Simeon; Jemuel and Jamen, and Ohad; and Jachin, and Zohar, and Shaul the son of a Canaanitish woman."[111]

(Jasher and the Legends) "and Simeon his brother took Dinah for a wife, and she bare unto him Memuel, Yamin, Ohad, Jachin, and Zohar, five sons. And he afterward came to Bunah the Canaanitish woman, the same is Bunah whom Simeon took captive from the city of Shechem, and Bunah was before Dinah and attended upon her, and Simeon came to her, and she bare unto him Saul."[112]

LEVI, born of Leah and Israel:

Isaac and Israel had been counseled by Abraham not to take a wife of Canaan or of strange nations. Levi, upon whom the priesthood blessings were bestowed, was given like counsel in these words,

"Therefore take for yourself a wife while you are still young, a wife who is free of blame or profanation, who is not from the race of alien nations."[113]

(From Jasher and the Legends) "And Levi and Issachar went to the land of the east, and they took unto themselves for wives the daughters of Jobab the son of Yoktan, the son of Eber; and Jobab the son of Yoktan had two daughters; the name of the elder was Adinah, and the name of the younger was Aridah. And Levi took Adinah, and Issachar took Aridah, and they came to the land of Canaan, to their father's house, and Adinah bare unto Levi Gershon, Kehath and Merari; three sons."[114]

(From Genesis) "And the sons of Levi; Gershon, Kohath and Merari"[115]

(The Testament of Levi) "Therefore when I took a wife I was twenty eight years old and her name was Melcha. And she conceived and bare a son, and I called his name Gershom, for we were sojourners in the land. And I saw concerning him, that he would not be in the first rank."

"And Kohath was born in the thirty fifth year of my life towards' the sunrise. And I saw a vision that he was standing on high in the midst of all the congregation. Therefore I called his name Kohath which is, beginning of majesty and instruction. And she bare me a third son in the fortieth year of my life; and since his mother bare him with difficulty, I called him Merari, that is my bitterness he also was like to die. And Jochebed (mother of Moses) was born in Egypt in my sixty fourth year, for I was renouned then in the midst of my brethren."[116]

JUDAH, born of Leah and Israel:

(From Genesis) "And it came to pass....that Judah went down from his brethren and turned in to a certain Adullamite whose name was Hirah. And Judah saw there a daughter of a certain Canaanite, whose name was Shuah; and he took her, and went in unto her. And she conceived, and bare a son; and he called his name Er. And she conceived again and bare a son; and she called his name Onan. And she yet again conceived, and bare a son, and called his name Shelah: And he was at Chezib, when she bare him."[117]

When about twenty years old Judah visited a certain Adullamite (Canaanite) identified by the Testament of Judah as Parsaba, king of Adullam. Judah had a chief herdsman Iram (Hirah) from the Adullamites. A feast was made by king Parsaba which Judah attended. Judah drank too much wine. He was also intoxicated by king Parzaba's daughter Alyath (Bathsua) and he slept with her. A marriage followed shortly thereafter. In retrospect Judah recognized it was a terrible mistake to have married her. Israel had not sanctioned his marriage to a Canaanite, a worshipper of idols, who held to those beliefs. Bathsua didn't want her sons to marry daughters who were not Canaanites, and took action to prevent children from being born from them.

Genesis reports the maturing of Judah and Bathsua's three sons, the marriage of two sons, the death of two sons and the death of Bathsua in six verses. How much time lapsed during this period is not known. No connection between the deaths of Judah's two sons and his wife is made in Genesis. Other writings offer some explanations. Bathsua was upset Er had married a descendant of Shem rather than Ham. She took action to prevent Er from having children by Tamar. And when Judah arranged for Onan to marry Tamar at Er's death Bathsua went into action again. Before Judah could marry his third son Shelah to Tamar, she arranged for him to be married to a Canaanite. Because of Bathsua's actions in these three circumstances Judah pronounced a curse on her and she died.[118]

(From Genesis) "and Judah took a wife for Er his firstborn, whose name was Tamar. And Er, Judah's firstborn, was wicked in the sight of the Lord; and the Lord slew him."[119]

His wickedness, according to Jasher was that he outwardly destroyed his seed. The Testament of Judah states that Er had been married to Tamar three days when the Lord slew him; Within another year Onan who filled in the place of his brother Er, was also dead, because Onan spilled his seed upon the ground and the Lord slew him also.

(From Genesis) "and Judah said unto Onan, Go in unto thy brother's wife, and marry her, and raise up seed to thy brother. And Onan knew that the seed should not be his; and it came to pass, when he went in unto his brother's wife, that he spilled it on the ground, lest he should give seed to his brother. And the thing which he did displeased the Lord: wherefore he slew him also."[120]

The Testament of Judah, as previously mentioned, holds Bathsua (Alyath), Judah's wife, mostly accountable for the actions of her two sons Er and Onan. Judah's third son Shelah wasn't quite old enough for marriage to Tamar. Tamar was asked to wait for Shelah to mature with intention to marry at that time. Tamar went to her father's house to wait. Genesis and Jasher imply that Judah was afraid if Shelah married Tamar he might die also, so Tamar was sent away, really, to be rid of her. The Testament of Judah, however, blames Bathsua for secretly arranging for Shelah to marry a Canaanite thereby frustrating Judah's plan to have Shelah marry Tamar, when he was old enough.

(From Genesis) Then said Judah to Tamar his daughter in law, Remain a widow at thy father's house, till Shelah my son is grown: for he said, Lest peradventure he die also, as his brethren did. And Tamar went and dwelt in her father's house. And in the process of time the daughter of Shuah, Judah's wife died; and Judah was comforted, and went up unto his sheepshearers to Timnath, he and his friend Hirah the Adullamite."[121]

(From the Testament of Judah) "I wanted to give Shelam to her also, but his mother would not allow it. She did this evil thing because

Tamar was not the daughter of Canaan as she was. ...while I was absent, she went off and brought from Canaan a wife for Shelam. When I realized what she had done, I pronounced a curse on her in the anguish of my soul, and she died in her wickedness, together with her children."[122]

Tamar was the daughter of Elam, the son of Shem, according to Jasher and of Aram, according to the Testament of Judah. Both Elam and Aram were sons of Shem, according to Genesis and Jasher, so Tamar was most likely a descendant of Shem. She expected to be married to Shelah waiting a couple of years for him, but it didn't happen. Shelah married a Canaanite. Twice widowed and with her father-in-law a widower, now, Tamar behaved strangely and wickedly by Israel's standards, but not so strangely or wickedly by Canaanite standards.

(From Genesis) "And it was told Tamar, saying, Behold thy father-in-law goeth up to Timnath to shear his sheep. And she put her widow's garments off from her, and covered her with a vail, and wrapped herself, and sat in an open place, which is by the way to Timnath; for she saw that Shelah was grown, and she was not given unto him to wife. When Judah saw her, he thought her to be an harlot; because she had covered her face."[123]

Tamar's behavior, according to the Testament of Judah, was in compliance with Amorite law.

(From the Testament of Judah) "After this, while Tamar was a widow she heard two years later that I was going to shear sheep. Decking herself in bridal array she sat at the entrance of the inn in the city of Eran, for there was a law among the Amorites that a woman who was widowed should sit in public like a whore (should sit in fornication seven days by the gate)."[124]

(From Genesis) "And he (Judah) turned unto her by the way, and said, Go to, I pray thee, let me come in unto thee; (for he knew not that she was his daughter in law.) And she said, what wilt thou give me, that thou mayest come in unto me? And he said, I will send thee a kid from the flock, And she said, Wilt thou give me a pledge, till thou send it? And he said, what pledge shall I give thee? And she said, Thy signet, and thy bracelets, and thy staff that is in thine hand. And he gave it her, and came in unto her, and she conceived by him. And she arose, and went away, and laid by her vail from her, and put on the garments of her widowhood."[125]

The Testament of Judah explains that Judah had been drinking when he saw Tamar, was enticed by her dress, left his ring, royal crown, and staff as a pledge until the kid from the flock was delivered.[126]

(From Genesis) "And Judah sent the kid by the hand of his friend the Adullamite, to receive his pledge from the woman's hand: but he found her not. Then he asked the men of that place, saying, where is the harlot, that was openly by the wayside? And they said, There was no harlot in this place. And he returned to Judah, and said, I cannot find her; and also the men of the place said, that there was no harlot in this place. And Judah said, Let her take it to her, lest we be shamed: behold, I sent this kid, and thou hast not found her."

"And it came to pass about three months after, that it was told Judah, saying, Tamar thy daughter in law hath played the harlot; and also, behold, she is with child by whoredom. And Judah said, Bring her forth, and let her be burnt."[127]

Apparently Tamar did not lose her composure under threat of death. She coolly responded by sending to Judah the surety Judah had left when he slept with her.

(From Genesis) "When she was brought forth, she sent to her father in law, saying, By the man, whose these are, am I with child: and she said, Discern, I pray thee, whose are these, the signet, and bracelets, and staff."[128]

Confronted with the evidence, Judah realized it was he who had impregnated her and said "She hath been more righteous than I."

(From Genesis) "And Judah acknowledged them, and said, She hath been more righteous than I; because that I gave her not to Shelah my son, And he knew her again no more. And it came to pass in the time of her travail, that, behold, twins were in her womb."[129]

Through these twins came the future kings of Israel.

(From Genesis) "And it came to pass, when she travailed, that the one put out his hand: and the midwife took and bound upon his hand a scarlet thread, saying, This came out first. And it came to pass, as he drew back his hand; that behold, his brother came out; and she said, How hast thou broken forth? this breach be upon thee: therefore his name was called Pharez. And afterward came out his brother, that had a scarlet thread upon his hand: and his name was called Zarah."[130]

When Judah went to Egypt with the rest of Israel's family he brought with him Shelah born of Bathsua and Pharez and Zarah born of Tamar, and two grandsons, Hezron and Hamul.[131]

ISSACHAR, born of Leah and Israel:

(From Genesis) "And the sons of Issachar: Tola and Phuvah, and Job and Shimron."[132]

(From Jasher) "Issachar went to the land of the east and....took....for a wife....the daughter of Jobab the son of Joktan, the son of Eber....and (her) name was Aridah....And Aridah bare unto Issachar Tola, Puvah, Job, and Shomron, four sons...."[133]

ZEBULUN, born of Leah and Israel:

(From Genesis) "And the sons of Zebulun; Sered, and Elon and Jahleel."[134]

(From Jasher) "And Zebulun went to Midian, and took for a wife Meriashah (Maroshah) the daughter of Molad, the son of Abida, the son of Midian, and brought her to the land of Canaan. And Merushah bare unto Zebulun Sered, Elan, Yatheel; three sons."[135]

(From Genesis) "These be the sons of Leah, which she bare unto Jacob in Padanaram with his daughter Dinah; and the souls of his sons and daughters were thirty and three."[136]

GAD, born of Zilpah and Israel:

(From Genesis) "And the sons of Gad; Ziphion, and Haagi, Shuni and Ezbon, Eri, and Arodi, and Areli."[137]

(From Jasher) "And Gad....went to Haran and took from thence the daughter of Amuram, the son of Uz, the son of Nahor a (wife). And these are the names of the daughters of Amuram, the elder was Merimah and the younger was Uzith....And Gad took Uzith....And Uzith bare unto Gad Zephion, Chagi, Shuni, Ezbon, Eri, Arodi, and Arali, seven sons."[138]

ASHER, born of Zilpah and Israel:

(From Genesis) "And the sons of Asher; Jimnah and Ishuah, and Isui and Beriah, and Serah their sister, and the sons of Beriah, Hebor and Malchiel."[139]

(From Jasher) "And Asher went forth and took Adon the daughter of Aphlal, the son of Hadad, the son of Ishmael, for a wife, and he brought her to the land of Canaan. And Adon the wife of Asher died in those days: she had no offspring. And it was after the death of Adon that Asher went to the other side of the river and took for a wife Hadurah the daughter of Abimael, the son of Eber, the son of Shem."

"And the young woman was of a comely appearance, and a woman of sense, and she had been the wife of Malkiel the son of Elam, the son of Shem. And Hadurah bare a daughter unto Malkiel, and he called her name Serach, and Malkiel died after this, and Hadurah went and remained in her father's house. And after the death of the wife of Asher he went and took Hadurah for a wife, and brought her to the land of Canaan, and Serach her daughter he also brought with them, and she was three years old,...and the damsel was of a comely appearance, and she went in the sanctified ways of the children of Jacob; she lacked nothing, and the Lord gave her wisdom and understanding. And Hadurah, the wife of Asher conceived, and bare unto him Yimnah, Yishvah, Yishiv, and Beriah, four sons."

"....And the children of Asher were Jimnah, Jishvah, Jishi, Beriah, and their sister Serach; and the sons of Beriah were Cheber and Malchiel."[140]

(From Genesis) "These are the sons of Zilpah whom Laban gave to Leah his daughter, and these she bare unto Jacob even sixteen souls."[141]

JOSEPH, born of Rachel and Israel:

(From Genesis) "The sons of Rachel Jacob's wife Joseph and Benjamin. And unto Joseph in the land of Egypt were born Manasseh and Ephraim, which Aseneth the daughter of Potiperah priest of On bare unto him."[142]

(From Jasher) "And the king sent to Potiphera the son of Ahiram, priest of On, and he took his young daughter Asenath and gave her unto Joseph for a wife. And the damsel was very comely, a virgin, one whom man had not known, and Joseph took her for a wife;....And Joseph's wife Asenath the daughter of Potiphera bare him two sons, Manasseh and Ephraim, and Joseph was thirty four years old when he begat them."[143]

BENJAMIN, born of Rachel and Israel:

(From Genesis) "And the sons of Benjamin were Belah and Becher, and Ashbel, Gera and Naaman, Ehi, and Rosh, Muppim and Huppim and Ard."[144]

(From Jasher) "And Jacob sent to Aram, the son of Zoba, the son of Terah, and he took for his son Benjamin, Mechalia the daughter of Aram, and she came to the land of Canaan to the house of Jacob; and Benjamin was ten years old when he took Mechalia the daughter of Aram for a wife. And Mechalia conceived and bare unto Benjamin Bela, Becher, Ashbel, Gera and Naaman, five sons, and Benjamin went afterward and took for a wife Aribath, the daughter of Shamron, the son of Abraham, in addition to his first wife, and he was eighteen years old, and Aribath bare unto Benjamin Achi, Vosh, Mupim, Chumpim, and Ord five sons."[145]

(From Genesis) "These are the sons of Rachel which were born to Jacob all the souls were fourteen."[146]

DAN, born of Bilhah and Israel:

(From Genesis) "And the sons of Dan; Hushim."[147]

(From Jasher) "And Dan went to the land of Moab and took for a wife Aphaleth, the daughter of Chamudan the Moabite, and he brought her to the land of Canaan. And Aphaleth was barren, she had no offspring, and God afterward remembered Aphaleth the wife of Dan, and she conceived and bare a son, and she called his name Chushim....And Chushim was dumb and deaf...."[148]

NAPHTALI, born of Bilhah and Rachel:

(From Genesis) "And the sons of Naphtali; Jahzeel and Guni, and Jezer and Shillem."[149]

(From Jasher) "And....Naphtali went to Haran and took from thence the daughter of Amuram the son of Uz, the son of Nahor for (a) wife. And these are the names of the daughters of Amuram; the name of the elder was Merimah....and Naphtali took Merimah and brought (her) to the land of Canaan to (his) father's house. And Merimah bare unto Naphtali Yachzeel, Guni, Jazer, and Shalem, four sons...."[150]

(From Genesis) "These are the sons of Bilhah which Laban gave unto Rachel his daughter, and she bare these unto Jacob; all the souls were seven. All the souls that came with Jacob into Egypt, which came out of his loins, besides Jacob's sons' wives, all the souls were three score and six; And the sons of Joseph, which were born him in Egypt, were two souls: all the souls of the house of Jacob which came unto Egypt were three score and ten."[151]

---

109. Genesis 46:8-9 KJV, MT, JST
110. Jasher XLV:1-2 see also Legends II:37; V, Yashar wa Yishlah 60b-89b
111. Genesis 46:10 KJV, MT, JST
112. Jasher XLV:2-3 see also Legends II:37-38; V, Yashar wa Yeshlah 60b-89b
113. Testament of Levi The Old Testament Pseudepigrapha I:p. 792;
    The Forgotten Books of Eden p. 230
114. Jasher XLV:5-6 see also Legends II:38-39; V, Yashar wa Yeshlah 8ba-90b
115. Genesis 46:11 KJV, MT, JST
116. Testament of Levi The Forgotten Books of Eden p. 230; The Old Testament Pseudepigrapha I p. 792
117. Genesis 38:1-5 KJV, MT, JST
118. Testament of Judah The Forgotten Books of Eden p 236, OTPp. 798

119. Genesis 38:6-7 KJV, MT, JST
120. Ibid 38:8-10
121. Ibid 38:11-12
122. The Testament of Judah The Old Testament Psuedepigrapha p. 798; The Forgotten Books of Eden 123. Genesis 38:13-15 KJV, MT, JST
124. The Testament of Judah The Old Testament Pseudepigrapha p. 798; The Forgotten Books of Eden p. 236
125. Genesis 38:16-19 KJV, MT, JST
126. The Testament of Judah The Old Testament Pseudepigrapha p. 798
127. Genesis 38:20-24 KJV, MT, JST
128. Ibid 38:25 KJV, MT, JST
129. Ibid 38:26-27 KJV, MT, JST
130. Ibid 38:28-30 KJV, MT JST
131. Ibid 46:12
132. Ibid 46:13
133. Jasher XLV:5-7 see also Legends II:38-39; V, Yashar Wa Yesheb
134. Genesis 46:14 KJV, MT, JST
135. Jasher XLV:9-20 see also Legends II:39
136. Genesis 46:15 KJV, MT, JST
137. Ibid 46:16
138. Jasher XLV:9-11 see also Legends II:39; V Yashar Wa Yesheb 80a
139. Genesis 46:17 KJV, MT, JST
140. Jasher XLV:12-18, LIX:16 see also Legends II:39; V Yashar Wa Yesheb 80a-90b
141. Genesis 46:18 KJV, MT, JST
142. Genesis 46:19-20 KJV, MT, JST
143. Jasher XLIX:36-37; L:15
144. Genesis 46:21 KJV, MT, JST
145. Jasher XLV:21-22 see also Legends II:39; V Yashar Wa Yesheb 80a-90b
146. Genesis 46:22 KJV, MT, JST
147. Ibid 46:23 KJV, MT, JST
148. Jasher XLV 7-8 LVI:63 see also Legends II:38-39; V Yashar Wa Yesheb 80a-90b
149. Genesis 46:24 KJV, MT, JST
150. Jasher XLV:9-11 see also Legends II:39; V Yashar Wa Yesheb 80a-90b
151. Genesis 46:25-27 KJV, MT, JST

CHAPTER VIII

JOSEPH'S EXPERIENCES IN PRISON

We return now to Joseph's experiences in prison while his brothers were marrying and having families. Although Joseph denied having tried to force Zelicah to lay with him or do anything like unto it, he did not condemn her for what she did, nor did he describe the exact circumstances. Rather, he commended all his affairs to God and silently underwent the bonds and distress he was in, firmly believing that God, who knew the cause of his affliction and the truth of the facts, would be more powerful than those who inflicted the punishments upon him. The correctness of this position was soon borne out.

A report from Antiquities:

"for the keeper of the prison taking notice of his care and fidelity in the affairs he had set him about, and the dignity of his countenance, relaxed his bonds, and thereby made his heavy calamity lighter and more supportable to him: he also permitted him to make use of a diet better than that of the rest of the prisoners."[152]

And from Genesis:

"And Joseph's master took him, and put him into the prison, a place where the kings prisoners were bound: and he was there in the prison. But the Lord was with Joseph, and shewed him mercy, and gave him favour in the sight of the keeper of the prison. And the keeper of the prison committed to Joseph's hand all the prisoners that were in the prison, and whatsoever they did there, he was the doer (overseer) of it. The keeper of the prison looked not to anything that was under his hand because the Lord was with him, and that which he did, and the Lord made it to prosper."[153]

Joseph was imprisoned at about age eighteen and was not released until age thirty some twelve years later, after he had interpreted the Pharaoh's dreams. He had interpreted the dreams of the Pharaoh's chief butler and baker two years prior to the Pharaoh's. This would indicate that Joseph had been in prison ten years before he interpreted the dreams of the butler and the baker. Little is reported of these ten years in Joseph's life. Part of this time Zelicah came to the prison and tried to persuade him to give in to her. He would not be persuaded and she actually gave up.

It was during these years in prison that Joseph gained the respect of the keeper of the prison. Undoubtedly he thought of his circumstances, having plenty of time available for reflection. His relationship to the Lord God Jehovah and his feelings toward Him are described in the Testament of Joseph:

"I have seen in my life, envy and death, yet I went not astray, but perservered in the truth of the Lord. These my brethren hated me but the Lord loved me:

They wished to slay me, but the God of my fathers guarded me:

They let me down into a pit, and the Most High brought me up again:

I was sold into slavery, and the Lord of all made me free:
I was taken into captivity and His strong hand succoured me:
I was beset with hunger, and the Lord Himself nourished me:
I was alone, and God comforted me:
I was sick and the Lord visited me:
I was in prison, and my God showed favor unto me:
In bonds, and he released me: Slandered, and he pleaded my cause:
Bitterly spoken against by the Egyptians and he delivered me:
Envied by my fellow slaves and He exalted me..."[154]

While thus imprisoned, but in charge of the prisoners there, Joseph eventually received into his hands the Pharaoh's chief butler and chief baker, each of whom had fallen out of favor with the Pharaoh.

(From Genesis) "And it came to pass after these things, that the butler of the king of Egypt and his baker had offended their lord, the king of Egypt. And Pharaoh was wroth against two of his officers, against the chief of the butlers and against the chief of the bakers. And he put them in ward in the house of the captain of the guard, into the prison the place where Joseph was bound. And the captain of the guard charged Joseph with them, and he served them: and they continued a season in ward."[155]

Genesis does not indicate what the butler and the baker did to incure the wrath of the Pharaoh and why they were imprisoned. Other writings furnish probable reasons. The butler had served the Pharaoh and those that ate at his table, wine which was found to have flies in it. The baker had brought for the Pharaoh et al to eat bread with stones of nitire (small pebbles) in it. More importantly, the butler allegedly tried to poison the Pharaoh. For their carelessness and alleged crimes the Pharaoh had them cast into the prison.[156]

They were placed in Joseph's charge. He noticed the butler and the baker were downcast one day, and asked them why. They each had had dreams, they said, which they could not understand. Joseph invited them to share these dreams with him. They did so, and Joseph interpreted them through the gift and power of God.

(From Genesis) "And they dreamed a dream both of them, each man his dream in one night, each man according to the interpretation of his dream, the butler and the baker of the king of Egypt, which were bound in the prison. And Joseph came in unto them in the morning, and looked upon them, and, behold, they were sad. And he asked Pharaoh's officer's that were with him in the ward of his lord's house, saying, wherefore look ye so sadly today? And they said unto him, We have dreamed a dream, and there is no interpreter of it. And Joseph said unto them, Do not intepretations belong to God? tell me them, I pray you."

"And the chief butler told his dream to Joseph, and said to him, In my dream, behold, a vine was before me; And in the vine were three branches: And it was as though it budded, and her blossoms shot forth; and the clusters thereof brought forth ripe grapes: And Pharaoh's cup was in my hand: and I took the grapes and pressed them into Pharaoh's cup and I took Pharaoh's cup, and I gave the cup unto Pharaoh's hand. And Joseph said unto him, This is the interpretation of it:

The three branches are three days: Yet within three days shall Pharaoh lift up thine head, and restore thee unto thy place: and thou shalt deliver Pharaoh's cup into his hand, after the former manner when thou wast his butler.

"But think on me when it shall be well with thee, and show kindness, I pray thee, unto me, and make mention of me unto Pharaoh, and bring me out of this house: For indeed I was stolen away out of the land of the Hebrews: and here also have I done nothing that they should put me into the dungeon."

"When the chief baker saw that the interpretation was good, he said unto Joseph, I also was in my dream, and behold, I had three white baskets on my head: And in the uppermost basket there was of all manner of bake meats for Pharaoh; and the birds did eat them out of the basket upon my head. And Joseph answered and said, This is the interpretation thereof: The three baskets are three days: Yet within three days shall Pharaoh lift up thy head from off thee, and shall hang thee on a tree; and the birds shall eat thy flesh from off thee."

"And it came to pass the third day, which was Pharaoh's birthday, that he made a feast unto all his servants. And he lifted up the head of the chief butler and of the chief baker among his servants. And he restored the chief butler unto his butlership again; and he gave the cup into Pharaoh's hand: But he hanged the chief baker: as Joseph had interpreted to them. yet did not the chief butler remember Joseph but forgat him."[157]

Note that Joseph possessed the gifts of prophecy and interpretation of dreams even while imprisoned. He blessed the lives of others through it but had not power to release himself from prison. He relied on the Pharaoh to do that, and therefore pled with the butler to put in a good word for him. The butler forgot him, but the Lord didn't. The Lord God Jehovah had other plans. Working through the Pharaoh two years later, Jehovah not only obtained Joseph's release, but exalted him within the Pharaoh's kingdom, thereby setting the stage for Israel to come to Egypt with his family during the famine and thereby fulfill the prophecies of Abraham.

Other writings attributed the butler's failure to remember Joseph to the Pharaoh as requested, to the Lord, who supposedly, punished Joseph because he trusted in man at least temporarily, and not in the Lord.[158]

It was during Joseph's final two years in prison that Isaac, his grandfather died. Prior to his death he blessed Israel and Esau and their posterity.

---

152. Antiquities Book II, V:1
153. Genesis 39:20-23 KJV, MT, JST
154. Testament of Joseph, Forgotten Books of Eden p. 259-260
155. Genesis 40:1-4 KJV, MT, JST
156. Jasher XVI:1-20 see also Legends II p. 60-61
157. Genesis 40:5-23 KJV, MT, JST
158. Jasher XLVI:19 see also Legends II:63; V Yashar Wa Yesheb

CHAPTER IX

ISAAC'S FINAL BLESSING, HIS DEATH AND BURIAL

Isaac's death approached in the 120th year of Israel's life and in the 29th year of the life of Joseph. Joseph was in prison in Egypt. Israel and his eleven sons and their families were with Isaac in Hebron. Esau and his sons, in Seir, received word that Isaac was about to die. They came to Canaan. Isaac requested Jacob (Israel) to come forward with his eleven sons. Isaac embraced, kissed them and invoked Abraham's blessing upon each one. The blessing included increase in their seed like the stars of heaven for number. Isaac also blessed Esau's sons.

Isaac admonished Israel to:

"teach thy children and thy children's children to fear the Lord, and to go in the good way which will please the Lord thy God, for if you keep the ways of the Lord and his statutes the Lord will also keep unto you his covenant with Abraham, and will do well with you and your seed all the days."[159]

Isaac then gave up the ghost and died. He was gathered unto his people and buried by his sons Esau and Jacob (Israel), in the cave of Machpelah along side Abraham, Sarah, Rebecca and Leah. Twenty seven years later Jacob (Israel) was also buried there.

Isaac was mourned as Abraham was, and the kings of Canaan showed him great honor at his death. Israel's and Esau's sons went barefooted round about, walking and lamenting on the way. They buried Isaac with very great honor as at the funeral of kings.

At the death of Isaac, he left his cattle and his possessions, land and all belonging to him to Esau and Israel. Isaac's estate was divided into two parts by Israel. Esau was invited to choose which part he was to take. One part was the land, the other part included riches, cattle and flocks. Esau was offered one or the other.

Esau counseled with Nebayoth, son of Ishmael. They reasoned that the land was really in control of the Canaanites, who dwelt securely there.

Better to take the riches, cattle and flocks and leave the land to Israel, they thought. Esau selected the riches, cattle and flocks and took them all back to Seir leaving the land to Israel as his inheritance.

Included in Israel's inheritance, then, was the cave of Machpelah the burial place of Abraham, Sarah, Isaac, Rebecca and Leah and where Israel later was buried. Also included in Israel's portion of the estate settlement was the land of Canaan and all the cities of the Hittites, the Hivites, and Jebusites, the Ammonites, the Perizzites and the Gergashites, all the seven nations from the river of Egypt unto the river Euphrates.

The city of Hebron, Kireatharba, and the cave which is in it did Jacob buy from Esau.

All these things were written down in a book of purchase, signed and testified to with four faithful witnesses. Jacob (Israel) took the book of purchase and the signatures, the commandment and the statutes and the revealed book, and he placed them in an earthen vessel in order that they remain a long time, and he delivered them into the hands of his children.

While generally not recognized as being the stature as Abraham, Isaac was certainly one of the great men of all the earth.

It has been written that Isaac:

- was born at a time set by the Lord God Jehovah Himself
- was also named by Him
- received revelation from God
- was a friend, servant and prophet of God

- received the priesthood or power to act for God and conferred it upon Jacob
- taught Levi in the law of the Priesthood
- bestowed his blessings upon Levi and Judah while Joseph was in Egypt
- was very much a proscelyte/missionary
- wore priestly garments
- loved the Lord God Jehovah with all his heart, offered sacrifices often and had no other gods before him.
- loved his neighbor, gave to the poor of Gerar
- honored his father and mother
- did not kill, commit adultery, steal, covet, bear false witness or take the name of the Lord in vain
- was willing to give all he had, for and to the Lord including himself as a sacrifice

In summary, Isaac lived a righteous life, kept the covenants he had made with God, and passed all the tests put to him including the Akedah. For his efforts Isaac was granted his exaltation, and he Isaac, also sitteth upon his celestial throne. "Isaac did none other things than that which (he was) commanded, (he has) entered into his exaltation according to (God's) promises and sit/s upon thrones...."[161]

---

159. Jasher XLVII:8
160. Jasher XLVII:15-29
161. Doctrine & Covenants 132:37

Chapter X

JOSEPH INTERPRETS THE PHARAOH'S DREAM

With the passing of Isaac the mantle of leadership for the Lord's covenant people fell upon Israel. The Lord had tested, tried and prepared Israel for the call through forty years of adversity while in Haran and in Canaan. Unknown to Israel at the time, the Lord was already grooming his future prophet, Joseph. He also was being tested through adversity, first, being sold by his brothers, and second while falsely imprisoned a period of at least twelve years. His imprisonment ended as a result of correctly interpreting the Pharaoh's dreams.

(From Genesis) "And it came to pass at the end of two full years the Pharaoh dreamed and behold, he stood by the river. And behold, there came up out of the river seven well favoured kine and fat fleshed; and they fed in a meadow. And, behold, seven other kine came up after them out of the river, ill favoured and lean fleshed; and stood by the other kine upon the brink of the river. And the ill favoured and lean fleshed kine did eat up the seven well favoured and fat kine. So Pharaoh awoke."

"And he slept and dreamed the second time: and, behold, seven ears of corn came up upon one stalk, rank and good. And, behold, seven thin ears and blasted with the east wind sprung up after them. And the seven thin ears devoured the seven rank full ears. And Pharaoh awoke, and, behold it was a dream."

"And It came to pass in the morning that his spirit was troubled: And he sent and called for all the magicians of Egypt, and all the wise men thereof: And Pharaoh told them his dream: but there was none that could interpret them unto Pharaoh."[162]

The reader is left to ponder what interpretations the magicians and wisemen gave to these dreams and why the Pharaoh rejected them. Antiquities reports that the wisest men among the Egyptians hesitated to give an interpretation of the Pharaoh's dreams and makes no mention of magicians being called upon.[163]

Jasher (Yashar) and the Legends, on the other hand, describe in considerable detail the interpretations placed upon the dreams of the Pharaoh by the magicians and the wise men of Egypt. The dreams were seen by them as separate events about to take place in the life of the Pharaoh.

The magicians claimed the first dream denoted Pharaoh would have seven daughters born to him who would all die during his lifetime. The second dream, they said, denoted Pharaoh would build seven cities which would all be destroyed during his lifetime. The Pharaoh rejected these interpretations and sent them away. He called for the wisest of men by way of proclamation and commanded them to come forward and interpret his dreams, otherwise suffer death. This proclamation brought to the Pharaoh an array of people who perceived themselves as wise men from Egypt and bordering nations. They, in turn, provided an array of interpretations being greatly divided among themselves as to what the dreams meant. Some said the seven good kine and good ears represented seven kings, princes, cities, wives, children, etc. all coming to a tragic end. None of them saw the two dreams as representing a single event. None of these interpretations pleased the Pharaoh.

> (From Jasher) "And the king (Pharaoh) knew in his wisdom that they did not altogether speak correctly in all these words, for this was from the Lord to frustrate the words of the wise men of Egypt, in order that Joseph might go forth from the house of confinement, and in order that he should become great in Egypt."[164]

Frustrated and angry with the inability of the magicians and wise men to interpret these dreams to his satisfaction, the Pharaoh sent out a proclamation that all these magicians and wise men were to be slain. It was at this point the chief butler reportedly came forward and related his experience in prison where Joseph had correctly interpreted his dream. Merod, the name ascribed to the chief butler, then related the dream of the chief baker and his own dream to the Pharaoh and gave Joseph's inter-pretations of them, the correctness of which was borne out by the Pharaoh's subsequent actions. Merod pled with the Pharaoh to seek Joseph's interpretation of his dreams and to defer the slaughter of the magicians and wise men until he had heard from Joseph. The Pharaoh agreed, stayed his order for the wise men and magicians to be slain, and sent for Joseph to be brought before him.[165]

The fate of the magicians and wise men of Egypt was thus in Joseph's hands. If he interpreted the dreams to the Pharaoh's satisfaction they would live. If not, they would be slaughtered, and perhaps he would also have been slain.

The Genesis account reads:

"Then spake the chief butler unto Pharaoh, saying I do remember my faults this day: Pharaoh was wroth with his servants, and put me in ward in the captain of the guards house, both me and the chief baker. And we dreamed a dream in one night, I and he: we dreamed each man according to the interpretation of his dream. And there was there with us a young man, an Hebrew, servant of the captain of the guard; and we told him, and he interpreted to us our dreams; to each man according to his dream he did interpret. And it came to pass, as he interpreted to us, so it was; me he restored unto mine office, and him he hanged."

"Then Pharaoh sent and called Joseph, and they brought him hastily out of the dungeon: And he shaved himself, and changed his raiment, and came in unto Pharaoh."[166]

The scene Joseph saw as he appeared before the Pharaoh dazzled him, for it was such a contrast to the prison which had been his home for twelve years. Joseph reportedly saw the Pharaoh sitting upon his throne dressed in princely garments amongst gold and rubies and emeralds and other precious stones, the throne being at the top of seventy steps. According to custom Joseph was treated as a common man and ascended to the third step with Pharaoh coming to sit on the fourth step. In this setting the Pharaoh related his dream to Joseph.[167]

The Genesis account reads:

"And Pharaoh said unto Joseph, I have dreamed a dream, and there is none that can interpret it: and I have heard say of thee, that thou canst understand a dream to interpret it. And Joseph answered Pharaoh saying, It is not in me: God shall give Pharaoh an answer in peace. And Pharaoh said unto Joseph, In my dream, behold, I stood upon the bank of the river: And, behold, there came up out of the river, seven kine, fatfleshed and well favoured; and they fed in a meadow: And behold, seven other kine came up after them, poor and very ill favoured and lean fleshed such as I never saw in all the land of Egypt for badness: And the lean and ill favoured kine did eat up the first seven fat kine: And when they had eaten them up, it could not be known that they had eaten them; but they were still ill favoured, as at the beginning, So I awoke."

"And I saw in my dream, and, behold, seven ears came up in one stalk, full and good: And, behold seven ears, withered, thin and blasted with the east wind, sprung up after them: And the thin ears devoured the seven good ears: And I told this unto the magicians; but there was none that could declare it to me."[168]

Note that Joseph had been in prison twelve years for something he didn't do. Free from bitterness and guile he had served as the Lord's conduit to bless the life of the butler, who should have been grateful, but was not. The Pharaoh now whose dreams press heavily upon him, was unable to obtain relief from what must have been the wisest of all of Egypt. Leaving no possibility unexamined he sought help from a slave who had been in prison twelve years. Joseph, confident the Lord would speak through him again, acknowledged that his gift came not from himself, but of God, declared: "It is not in me. God shall give Pharaoh an answer in peace."[169]

And from other reports:

"and Joseph answered Pharaoh saying, Let Pharaoh relate his dreams that he dreamed, surely the interpretations belong to God; And Pharaoh related his dreams to Joseph....And Joseph was then clothed with the spirit of God before the king, and he knew all the things that would befall the king from that day forward...."[170]

Joseph declared the two dreams to be a single dream and that the dreams showed the Pharaoh what God had chosen to do throughout the land: namely, there were to be seven years of plenty followed by seven years of severe famine.

(From Genesis) "And Joseph said unto Pharaoh, The dream of the Pharaoh is one. God hath showed Pharaoh what he is about to do. The seven good kine are seven years; and the seven good ears are seven years: the dream is one. And the seven thin and ill favoured kine that came up after them are seven years; and the seven empty ears blasted with the east wind shall be seven years of famine. This is the thing which I have spoken unto Pharaoh, what God is about to do he sheweth unto Pharaoh."

"Behold, there come seven years of great plenty through all the land of Egypt. And there shall arise after them seven years of famine; and the famine shall consume the land; And the plenty shall not be known in the land by reason of that famine following; for it shall be very grievous. And for that the dream was doubled unto Pharaoh twice, it is because the thing is established by God, and God will shortly bring it to pass."

"Now therefore let Pharaoh look out a man discreet and wise, and set him over the land of Egypt. Let Pharaoh do this, And let him appoint officers over the land, and take up the fifth part of the land of Egypt in the seven plenteous years, And let them gather all the food of those good years that come, and lay up corn under the hand of Pharaoh, and let them keep food in the cities, and that food shall be for store to the land against the seven years of famine, which shall be in the land of Egypt that the land perish not through the famine."

"And the thing was good in the eyes of Pharaoh, and in the eyes of all his servants."[171]

---

162. Genesis 41:1-8 see also Jasher XLVIII:1-29
163. Antiquities Book II, V:4
164. Jasher XVIII:1-25 see also Legends II 63-67; V Yashar Mikkez 94a-96b
165. Ibid XLVIII:26-39, see also Legends II:67; V Yashar Mikkez

166. Genesis 41:9-14 see also Jasher XLVIII:30-41
167. Jasher XVIII:42-48 see also Legends II 69; V Yasher Mikkez 95a
168. Genesis 41:15-24 KJV, MT, JST
169. Ibid 41:16 KJV, MT, JST
170. Jasher XLVIII:51-52 see also Legends II:69-70; V Yashar Mikkez 95a
171. Genesis 41:25-37 KJV, MT, JST

Chapter XI

A MAN DISCREET AND WISE

Joseph had proposed a major change in social policy for all Egypt, i.e. to save enough food during the upcoming seven years of plenty for a whole nation and to spare; and to feed some of the people of surrounding nations as well. The food saved was to be consumed during a subsequent seven year period of famine. Further, that twenty percent of the land should be set aside for production of the crops, the results of which were to be saved and stored for use during the future seven years of famine.

Such an undertaking undoubtedly required the help and cooperation of thousands of workers, millions of cubic feet of storage space, and thousands of acres of land. The Pharaoh and all his servants seemingly accepted Joseph's recommendations without question and proceeded to implement them. The Pharaoh asked if such a discreet and wise person could be found to implement these plans. He answered his own question by declaring Joseph was that discreet and wise person, and promptly appointed him as second in command with a charge to proceed.

There may well be more to the story than reported in Genesis as another report implies. Concluding his interpretation of the Pharaoh's dreams, Joseph declared:

(From Jasher) "Let all the inhabitants of the land be also ordered that they gather in, every man the produce of his field, of all sorts of food, during the seven good years, and that they place it in their stores, that it may be found for them in the days of the famine and that they may live upon it."[172]

The Pharaoh responded to Joseph's recommendations with a logical question, "who sayeth and who knoweth that thy words are correct."[173]

Joseph countered with an apparent prophecy not recorded in Genesis. He said that a sign would be given to confirm the truth of his words, namely, that the Pharaoh's wife was that day on the stools of delivery and that she would give birth to a son in whom the Pharaoh would rejoice. However, the Pharaoh's two year old son would simultaneously (or nearly so) die. Shortly after Joseph's departure from the presence of Pharaoh, word was received of the birth of a new son to the Pharaoh, followed by word his first born two year old son was found dead upon the ground. The news brought great lamentation and noise to the Pharaoh's house as they grieved over the loss of his first born. The Pharaoh then knew of the correctness of Joseph's words concerning the forthcoming seven years of plenty, followed by seven years of famine. He took comfort in his relationship with his new born son as Joseph had prophesied.[174]

The Pharaoh was convinced, but what of his subjects, and those in power around him? Were they able to accept Joseph as second in command over all Egypt without question? Such appointment of Joseph effectively downgraded many of the Pharaoh's most powerful subordinates.

Genesis reported simply: "And Pharaoh said unto Joseph, See, I have set thee over all the land of Egypt."[175] Then Pharaoh clothed Joseph with vestures of power and authority, including the use of the Pharaoh's ring, and Joseph rode in the second chariot. One wonders how the Pharaoh was able to do this without rumblings in the ranks.

Jasher and the Legends contain some explanations. They report that when the Pharaoh declared Joseph to be the discreet and wise one to head up the effort to save Egypt from the famine, there were many doubters who wanted further proof that Joseph should be appointed to that position. Apparently it was written in the laws of Egypt that the second in command must have a knowledge of and be able to speak all the languages of the sons of men. The number of languages of the day were seventy, according to the Masoretic Text of the Holy Scriptures, Jasher and the Legends. The doubters reasoned Joseph spoke only Hebrew and Egyptian and that the language requirement would automatically disqualify him. A test of Joseph's language ability was set for the following day.

The Pharaoh's subordinates still could not comprehend that Joseph was acting with gifts and powers delegated to him by the Lord God, and he Jehovah (Yahweh) would come to Joseph's aid. Thus he did. During the night ministering angels came and taught Joseph in these seventy languages and called his name Jehoseph. As was the custom, Joseph advanced toward the Pharaoh step by step, until he had advanced up all seventy steps. The gift of tongues had been given to Joseph by the Lord God. The Pharaoh's subordinates were convinced.[176]

The Genesis account:

> "And Pharaoh said unto Joseph, For as much as God hath shewed thee all this, there is none so discreet and wise as thou. Thou shalt be over my house, and according unto thy word shall all my people be ruled: Only in the throne will I be greater than thou. And Pharaoh said unto Joseph, See I have set thee over all the land of Egypt. And Pharaoh took off his ring from his hand, and put it upon Joseph's hand, and arrayed him in vestures of fine linen, and put a gold chain about his neck, and he made him to ride in the second chariot which he had and they cried before him, Bow the knee: and he made him ruler over all the land of Egypt."[177]

Jasher and the Legends elaborate. In addition to being arrayed in vestures of fine linen, with a golden chain around his neck and the Pharaoh's ring on his finger, a golden crown was put on Joseph's head. The Pharaoh commanded that great music be played with timbrels, harps, mecholoths, and nebalims, as thousands of musicians marched in the streets followed by thousands of warriors with glittering swords, and other thousands with protective gear about them. Women and damsels gazed at the great beauty of Joseph.

The road was perfumed with frankincense and cassia. Myrrh and aloes were scattered along the road. A chorus of twenty men declared with a loud voice:

> "Do you see this man whom the king (Pharaoh) has chosen to be his second? all the affairs of government shall be regulated by him, and

he that transgresses his orders, or that does not bow down before him to the ground, shall die, for he rebels against the king and his second.... (then) all the people of Egypt bowed down to the ground before Joseph....and rejoiced."

Seeing all this Joseph,

"lifted up his eyes to heaven, and called out and said, He raiseth the poor man from the dust, He lifteth up the needy from the dunghill, O Lord of Hosts, happy is the man who trusteth in thee."[178]

Joseph toured all Egypt as he continued to be introduced as the Pharaoh's second in command. The Pharaoh showered other gifts upon him; 3,000 talents of silver, 1,000 talents of gold, onyx stones, and bdellium. The citizenry gave Joseph golden ear-rings and different vessels of gold and precious stones which Joseph took and put in his treasury. The Pharaoh sent to Potipherah (Potiphera) the son of Ahiram, priest of On, and he took his young daughter Osnath (Asenath) and gave her unto Joseph for a wife.

Asenath was very comely, a virgin one whom man had not known, and Joseph took her for a wife. The Pharaoh changed Joseph's name to Zaphnath-paeneah, and gave him control over those who entered and departed from the land of Egypt.[179]

The Legends explained Joseph's new name given by the Pharaoh as follows: Zaphenath-paaneah,

"Zaddi, stands for Zafeh, seer; Pe for Podeh, redeemer; nun for Nabi, prophet; taw for Tomek, supporter; Pe for Poter, interpreter of dreams; Ain for Arum, clever; Nun for Nabren, discreet; Het for hakam, wise."[180]

Antiquities reports Joseph's new name to be Psothom Panech, given by Pharaoh out of regard for his prodigious degree of wisdom. The name denoted revealer of secrets i.e. a prophet.[181]

Interestingly, the Pharaoh's new name for Joseph Zaphnath-paneah, declared him to be a prophet, seer, and revelator. Such was Joseph in the eyes of Jehovah, his God, and in the eyes of the people.

(From Genesis) "And Pharaoh said unto Joseph, I am Pharaoh and without thee shall no man lift up his hand or foot in all the land of Egypt. And Pharaoh called Joseph's name Zaphnath-paaneah: And he gave him to wife Asenath, the daughter of Potipherah, priest of On. And Joseph went out over all the land of Egypt."[182]

Asenath was the daughter of Potipherah, or Petephres whom Antiquities and the Testament of Joseph declare to have been the same man as Joseph's master when he first came to Egypt. Jasher reports that Ahiram, Potipherah's father was the priest of On, rather than Potipherah.[183]

What a dramatic change the Lord wrought in Joseph's life! Twelve years was Joseph in prison from age eighteen to age thirty: From ragged and dirty prisoner he rose to second in command to the Pharaoh almost overnight.

In addition to all the honor given Joseph, previously mentioned, the Pharaoh gave him a hundred servants and purchased even more for him. Joseph built a very magnificent house like unto the house of kings, and a large temple to go with it, very elegant in appearance and conveniently located. All Egypt loved Joseph.

An army of more than 4,600 men was put together under Joseph's command. During his first year in his new role Joseph led these troops in battle to aid the Ishmaelites in their battles with the children of Tarshish. They subdued the children of Tarshish without losing a man.[184]

The seven years of plenty began.

(From Genesis) "And Joseph was thirty years old when he stood before Pharaoh king of Egypt. And Joseph went out from the presence of Pharaoh and went throughout all the land of Egypt."

"And in the seven plenteous years the earth brought forth by handfuls. And he gathered up all the food of the seven years, which were in the land of Egypt, and laid up food in the cities: the food of the field, which was round about every city, laid he up in the same. And Joseph gathered corn as the sand of the sea, very much, until he left numbering, for it was without number."

"And unto Joseph were born two sons before the years of famine came, which Asenath the daughter of Potipherah, priest of On bare unto him. And Joseph called the name of the firstborn Manasseh: For God, said he, hath made me forget all my toil, and all my fathers house. And the name of the second called he Ephraim: For God hath caused me to be fruitful in the land of my affliction."[185]

Antiquities reports Manasseh signified "forgetful" because Joseph's present happiness made him forget his former misfortunes, and Ephraim signified, "restored", because he was restored to the freedom of his forefathers.[186]

Ephraim and Manasseh are of special significance to the Latter Day Saints, for it is through Ephraim's posterity, they believe, the truth as it was known in Abraham, Isaac, Israel's and Joseph's day is being restored in our day. It is through Manasseh's posterity that the Book of Mormon was written and revealed to the world.

Manasseh and Ephraim were born to Joseph and Asenath in Joseph's thirty fourth year, according to Jasher, or in the fourth year of plenty.[187]

The Legends say that Manasseh and Ephraim were bred in chastity and fear of God by their father. They were wise, and well-instructed in all knowledge and in the affairs of state, so that they became the favorites of the court, and were educated with the royal princes.[188]

Jasher and the Legends report that the people laid up corn and grain in abundance, but their methods of storage differed from Joseph's. Joseph had soil of the field brought with his corn and grains, had ashes and earth strewn on the garnered food from the very soil on which it had been grown. He also preserved the grain in the ear and took precautions to guard against rot and mildew.[189]

---

172. Jasher XLVIII:60
173. Ibid XLVIII:62

174. Ibid XLVIII:63-66 see also Legends II:70-71; V Yashar Mikkez 96b
175. Genesis 41:41 KJV, MT, JST
176. Jasher XVIX:1-18 see also Legends II:71-72; V Yashar Mikkez 96b-97a
177. Genesis 41:39-43 KJV, MT, JST
178. Jasher XLIX:18-30 see also Legends 74; V Yashar Mikkez 97a
179. Ibid XLIX:21-36 see also Legends II:75; V Yashar Mikkez 97a-97b
180. Legends II:75-76
181. Antiquities Book II, VI:1
182. Genesis 41:44-45 KJV, MT, JST
183. Antiquities Book II, VI:1
184. Jasher XLIX:38-44, L:1-6 see also Legends II:77; V Yashar Mikkez 98a -98b
185. Genesis 41:46-53 KJV, MT, JST
186. Antiquities Book II, VI:1
187. Jasher L:7-15
188. Legends II, p. 77
189. Ibid II, p. 78

Chapter XII

AND THE SEVEN YEARS OF DEARTH BEGAN TO COME AND JOSEPH'S TEN BRETHREN WENT TO BUY CORN IN EGYPT.

(From Genesis) "And the seven years of plenteousness that was in the land of Egypt was ended. And the seven years of dearth began to come, according as Joseph had said: and the dearth was in all lands; but in all the land of Egypt there was bread. And when all the land of Egypt was famished, the people cried to Pharaoh for bread: and Pharaoh said unto all the Egyptians, Go unto Joseph; what he saith to you, do. And the famine was over all the face of the earth: And Joseph opened all the storehouses, and sold unto the Egyptians; and the famine waxed sore in the land of Egypt, And all countries came into Egypt to Joseph for to buy corn; because that the famine was sore in all lands."[190]

Jasher and the Legends add that the people of Egypt opened their own stores of food, and found them full of vermin, rotting and unfit to eat. Apparently the example the prophet Joseph set in storing food had not been followed. They sought Joseph's help. He called upon the Egyptians to give up their idols and worship the living God and say, "Blessed is He who giveth bread unto all flesh." They ignored Joseph's admonition and betook themselves to Pharaoh seeking bread.

The Pharaoh took them to task for failure to follow Joseph's orders to store food during the seven years of plenty. They replied they had done so, but that their stores were full of vermin, rotted and unfit to eat. The Pharaoh was affrighted and urged them to "Go unto Joseph; what he saith to you, do". Again Joseph appealed to them to worship the living God and as evidence of their commitment to Him, be circumcised and enter into a covenant with Him.

Back to the Pharaoh they went saying Joseph had spoken roughly unto them, "circumcise yourselves". They also blamed him for the vermin and rot in their own food stores claiming Joseph willed it. Answering them the Pharaoh declared:

> "O ye fools, if his word hath power over the grain, making it to rot when he desireth it to rot, then also we must die, if it so be his wish concerning us. Go, therefore unto him, and do as he bids you."[191]

The Egyptians returned again unto Joseph crying for food. He opened up his own stores and the stores of the Pharaoh and sold to them.

The famine spread to adjacent lands. They were compelled to seek food in Egypt. Joseph had already been given power over those who entered or departed from Egypt. With word that the famine was already in Canaan, Joseph knew it was a matter of time before his brethren would come to Egypt to buy corn. The rich could not send their servants with many beasts of burden. Each must send his sons instead. Food to be purchased was limited to what could be loaded on his own beast. Joseph also required those who came to buy corn must supply the name of their fathers. The records of those buying corn were to be brought to Joseph for review. In this way he would know when his brethren arrived in Egypt, among the hundreds, perhaps thousands who would come.[192]

Returning to Genesis:

> "Now when Jacob saw that there was corn in Egypt, Jacob said unto his sons, why do ye look one to another? And he said, Behold, I have heard that there is corn in Egypt: get you down thither and buy corn for us from thence; that we may live and not die. And Joseph's ten brethren went to buy corn in Egypt. But Benjamin, Joseph's brother, Jacob sent not with his brethren; for he said, Lest peradventure mischief might befall him."[193]

Jacob's reference to Egypt must have pricked the consciences of his ten sons. They undoubtedly remembered they had sold Joseph into Egypt and lied to their father, making it appear Joseph was dead. Now, father Israel commanded them to go to the very land where Joseph was taken as a slave, and where he might still be alive. No wonder they looked at one another and hesitated to go to Egypt. They agreed to go, however, and started on their journey.

While on the road they reportedly repented of what they had done to Joseph and vowed to find and bring him back with them. Israel had counseled his sons to enter different gates so as to not attract attention i.e. that they were all sons of the same man.

Joseph's servants brought him the records of those who had entered into the gates of his city each evening. He recognized the names of his brethren, sons of Israel. He ordered all stores closed but one, forcing his brethren to purchase from it.

Unknown to Joseph, the first order of his brother's business was to try to find him they had sold. They delayed the purchase of corn and looked for Joseph instead. Because of Joseph's great beauty they reasoned he would have been sold to a house of harlots. They searched three days for him in these places, but did not find him.

In the meantime, Joseph was puzzled. His brethren had been in Egypt three days, and had not yet shown up to purchase corn from the only store that was open. He sent sixteen servants to try to find them. Four of these servants found the sons of Israel searching for Joseph in one of the houses of harlots. The ten brothers were brought before Joseph, who was sitting on his throne in the temple dressed in princely garments, a crown of gold upon his head and mighty servants round about. Joseph's brothers did not recognize him.[194]

Back to Genesis:

> "And the sons of Israel came to buy corn among those that came for the famine was in the land of Canaan. And Joseph was governor over the land, and he it was that sold to all the people of the land: and Joseph's brethren came, and bowed down themselves before him with their faces to the earth....And Joseph knew his brethren, but they knew not him."[195]

"From where come ye?" Joseph queried. "From the land of Canaan to buy food", they replied. Joseph asked why they didn't all come through the same gate to the city rather than through ten separate gates. Spies, Joseph pretended, to see the nakedness of the land. His brothers protested, saying no, that they had just come to buy corn, explaining that Father Israel had counselled them to come through separate gates, fearing the Egyptians might be angry if ten brothers all wanted to buy corn. Why have you not yet bought corn, seeing you have been in Egypt three days, Joseph countered. Because, they said, we were trying to find our brother whom we thought had been sold as a slave into Egypt.

Why do you look for him in a house of harlots?, queried Joseph. His brothers thought he would have been sold to such a place because of his great beauty. Joseph countered, saying, he knew that a house of harlots was not the place for a son of a Hebrew, even of Abraham, and again accused them of being spies. The questioning continued. What would they do if their brother's master wanted a high price? The price would be paid, they replied. What if their brother were not for sale, what would they do? Take him by force and slay his master, was the reply. Still claiming his brothers were spies Joseph sought to test them further by demanding they bring Benjamin to him. Joseph kept Simeon to assure their return to Egypt.[196]

The Genesis account:

"And Joseph saw his brethren, and he knew them; but made himself strange unto them, and spake roughly unto them; and he said unto them, whence come ye: And they said, From the land of Canaan to buy food. And Joseph knew his brethren, but they knew not him. And Joseph remembered the dreams which he had dreamed of them, (i.e. that they would make obesience to him) and said unto them, ye are spies; to see the nakedness of the land ye are come."

"And they said unto him, Nay, nay lord, but to buy food are thy servants come. We are all one man's sons, we are true men, thy servants are no spies. And he said unto them, Nay but to see the nakedness of the land ye are come. And they said, Thy servants are twelve brethren, the sons of one man in the land of Canaan; and, behold, the youngest is this day with our father, and one is not, And Joseph said unto them, That is it that I spake unto you, saying, ye are spies."

"Hereby ye shall be proved: By the life of Pharaoh ye shall not go forth hence, except your youngest brother come thither. Send one of you, and let him fetch your brother, and ye shall be kept in prison, that your words may be proved, whether there by any truth in you: or else by the life of Pharaoh surely ye are spies. And he put them all together into ward three days. And Joseph said unto them the third day, this do, and live; for I fear God: If ye be true men, let one of your brothers be bound in the house of your prison: go ye, carrying corn for the famine of your houses: But bring your youngest brother unto me; So shall your words be verified and ye shall not die. And they did so."[197]

Reuben had spoken in their behalf as Joseph accused them of being spies. Antiquities reported Reuben's defense of the actions of Israel's ten sons:

"We come not hither....with any unjust design, nor in order to bring any harm to the kings affairs; we only want to be preserved as supposing your humanity might be a refuge for us from the miseries which our country labors under, we having heard you proposed to sell corn not only to your country men, but to strangers also, and that you determined to allow that corn in order to preserve all that want it; but that we are brethren and of the same common blood....our father's name is Jacob, a Hebrew man, who had twelve of us for his sons by four wives;...."[198]

When Joseph required of his brothers that they bring Benjamin to Egypt, they wept. A general sadness seized them and they repented of what they had done to Joseph and concluded what was about to happen was the punishment of a just God. When Joseph saw them with broken hearts and contrite spirits he himself fell into tears. They knew not that Joseph understood them. They thought he was Egyptian since he spoke through an interpreter. Not being willing that they should see him cry, Joseph retired to another room and wept.

Simeon was selected to serve as surety while Joseph's brethren returned to Canaan to bring Benjamin as demanded. Simeon, wild, ferocious and strong, was not easily subdued. It was Manasseh, Joseph's five year old son, who by some miracle, subdued him.[199]

Their sacks were filled with corn. Unknown to them, their money was placed in the mouths of their sacks, and the nine sons of Israel began the return journey to Canaan.

The Genesis account:

"And they said to one another, We are verily guilty concerning our brother, in that we saw the anguish of his soul, when he besought us, and we would not hear; therefore is this distress upon us. And Reuben answered them, saying, spake I not unto you, saying, Do not sin against the child; and ye would not hear? therefore, behold, also his blood is required."

"And they knew not Joseph understood them; for he spake unto them by an interpreter. And he turned himself about after them, and wept; and returned to them, and communed with them, and took from them Simeon, and bound him before their eyes."

"Then Joseph commanded to fill their sacks with corn, and to restore every man's money into his sack, and to give them provision for the way: and thus did he unto them. And they laded their asses with the corn, and departed thence. And as one of them opened his sack to give his ass provender in the inn he espied his money; for behold it was in the sacks mouth. And he said unto his brethren, my money is restored; and lo, it is even in my sack: and their hearts failed them, and they were afraid, saying one to another, what is this that God hath done unto us?"[200]

Levi, reportedly, was the brother who found his money returned in the mouth of his sack. After asking themselves the question, "what is this that God hath done unto us", they, as sons of Abraham, Isaac, and Israel, wondered why the Lord would deliver them unto the hands of the king of Egypt. Reuben reminded them of his advice which went unheeded in years past, and Judah answered saying, "Surely we are guilty sinners before the Lord our God in having sold our brother, our own flesh." They tarried overnight in this inn, rose up early the next morning, laded their asses and went on home to Canaan and to their father Israel's house.[201]

(From Genesis) "And they came unto Jacob their father in the land of Canaan, and told him all that befell unto them....And it came to pass as they emptied their sacks, that behold, every man's bundle of money was in his sack: And when both they and their father saw the bundles of money they were afraid."[202]

Israel reacted to all they said with some bitterness of soul, wondering aloud if his own sons had somehow set out to destroy him and bring him down to his grave in sorrow. He lamented the loss of Joseph, and the imprisonment of Simeon in Egypt. He simply refused to let his nine sons take Benjamin back to Egypt fearing he also would be lost. The pinch of hunger would soon change his mind, however. Judah so advised his brethren to wait until the corn they had brought was consumed. He believed father Israel would relent and allow Benjamin to be taken with them in order to assuage the hunger of his children and grandchildren.[203]

(From Genesis) "And Jacob their father said unto them, me have ye bereaved of my children: Joseph is not, and Simeon is not and ye will take Benjamin away: all these things are against me. And Reuben spake unto his father saying, Slay my two sons, if I bring him not to thee: deliver him into my hand, and I will bring him to thee again. And he said, my son shall not go down with you: for his brother is dead, and he is left alone: if mischief befall him by the way in the which ye go, then shall ye bring down my gray hairs with sorrow to the grave."

"And the famine was sore in the land, And it came to pass, when they had eaten up the corn which they had brought out of Egypt, their father said unto them, go again, buy us a little food."[204]

Jasher indicates it took about fourteen months to consume the food they had previously brought from Egypt. Israel's grandchildren pled for bread. His compassion was aroused. Israel wept over them and their hunger. He called his sons together again and asked them to go again to Egypt to buy more food. Judah reminded father Israel that Benjamin was to go with them as required by the Pharaoh's second. Defending what they had done Judah responded:

(From Genesis) "And Judah spake unto him, saying, The man did solemnly protest unto us, saying, Ye shall not see my face, except your brother be with you. If thou wilt send our brother with us, we will go down and buy thee food: But if thou wilt not send him, we will not go down: for the man said unto us, ye shall not see my face, except your brother be with you."

"And Israel said, wherefore dealt ye so ill with me, as to tell the man whether ye had yet a brother? And they said, The man asked us straitly of our state, and of our kindred, saying, Is your father yet alive? have ye another brother? and we told him according to the tenor of these words: could we certainly know that he would say, Bring your brother down?"

"And Judah said unto Israel his father, send the lad with me, and we will arise and go, that we may live, and not die, both we, and thou, and also our little ones. I will be surety for him; of my hand shalt thou require him: if I bring him not unto thee, and set him before thee, then let me bear the blame forever: For except we had lingered, surely now we had returned this second time."[205]

---

190. Genesis 41:53-57 KJV, MT, JST
191. Legends II:p. 76-79; V Yashar Mikkez 98b-99a; Jasher L:18-39
192. Jasher L:18-39 see also Legends II p. 76-79; V Yashar Mikkez 98a-99a
193. Genesis 42:1-4 KJV, MT, JST
194. Jasher LI:1-20 see also Legends II:79-82; V Yashar Mikkez 98a-99a
195. Genesis 42:5-8 KJV, MT, JST
196. Jasher LI:20-35 see also Legends II:85; V Yashar Mikkez 101a
197. Genesis 42:7-20 KJV, MT, JST
198. Antiquities II, VI:3-4
199. Ibid II:VI:3-4; Jasher LI:35-47 see also Legends II: p. 86-87
200. Genesis 42:21-28 KJV, MT, JST; Jasher lI:48-52, 53
201. Jasher LI:48-52, 53 see also Legends II:87; V Yashar Mikkez 101b-102a
202. Genesis 42:29-35 KJV, MT, JST
203. Jasher LII:1-6, see also Legends II:88; V Yashar Mikkez 102a-102b
204. Genesis 42:36-38 43:1-2 KJV, MT, JST
205. Genesis 43:3-10 KJV, MT, JST

CHAPTER XIII

O LORD GOD OF HEAVEN AND EARTH, REMEMBER THY COVENANT WITH OUR FATHER ABRAHAM AN DEAL KINDLY WITH MY SONS

Israel relented. He instructed them to take double money with them to repay that which was returned in the mouths of their sacks previously, and to take of honey, balms, spices, nut and almonds (apparently trees with deep roots, bushes, etc. still produced some food, and honey, hard as stone, in spite of the famine) as a present for the governor of Egypt. Benjamin was to accompany them as required.

(From Genesis) "And their father Israel said unto them, If it must be so now, do this; take of the best fruits of the land in your vessels, and carry down the man a present, a little balm, and a little honey, spices, and myrrh, nuts and almonds: And take double money in your hand: and the money that was brought again in the mouth of your sacks, carry it again in your hand; per adventure it was an oversight: Take also your brother, and arise, go again unto the man: And God Almighty give you mercy before the man, that he may send away your brother, and Benjamin. If I be bereaved of my children, I am bereaved."[206]

However, before his son's departure for Egypt, Israel held family prayer. He spread forth his hands. He prayed to the Lord on account of his sons reportedly saying:

(From Jasher) "O Lord God of heaven and earth, remember thy covenant with our father Abraham, remember it with my father Isaac and deal kindly with my sons and deliver them not unto the hands of the king of Egypt; do it I pray thee O God for the sake of thy mercies and redeem all my children and rescue them from Egyptian power, and send them their two brothers. And all the wives of the sons of Jacob and their children lifted up their eyes to heaven, and they all wept before the Lord, and cried unto him to deliver their fathers from the hand of the king of Egypt."[207]

Israel reportedly sent a letter with them by way of Judah. He rehearsed his family history, from Abraham, and appealed for the safe return of his sons:

(From the Legends) "From thy servant Jacob, the son of Isaac, the grandson of Abraham, prince of God, to the mighty and wise king Zaphenath paneah, the ruler of Egypt, peace! I make known unto my lord the king that the famine is sore with us in the land of Canaan, and I have therefore sent my sons unto thee, to buy us a little food, that we may live, and not die."[208]

Israel knew not that he was addressing his own son Joseph, whom the Pharaoh had renamed Zaphenath paneah and whom the Pharaoh acknowledged as a prophet, seer and revelator of God.

Israel admitted it was he who had sent them through different gates so as not to attract attention, and denied that he had sent them as spies. He closed his letter with an appeal for the safe return of his sons.

(From the Legends) "I have said all now that is in my heart. My sons take their youngest brother down into Egypt with them, and do thou send them back to me in peace."[209]

Israel admonished his sons to take good care of Benjamin and not leave him out of their sight, either on the journey or after their arrival in Egypt.

(From Genesis) "And the men took that present, and they took double money in their hand, and Benjamin; and rose up, and went down to Egypt, and stood before Joseph."[210]

Upon reentering Egypt Israel's sons were again brought before Joseph the governor. They still did not recognize their brother.

(From Genesis) "And when Joseph saw Benjamin with them, he said to the ruler of his house, Bring these men home, and slay, and make ready; for these men shall dine with me at noon. And the man did as Joseph bade; and the man brought the men into Joseph's house. And the men were afraid, because they were brought into Joseph's house; and they said, Because of the money that was returned in our sacks at the first time are we brought in; that he may seek occasion against us, and fall upon us, and take us for bondmen, and our asses."

"And they came hear to the steward of Joseph's house, and they communed with him at the door of the house, and said, O sir, we came indeed down at the first time to buy food: And it came to pass, when we came to the inn, that we opened our sacks, and behold, every man's money was in the mouth of his sack, our money in full weight: and we have brought it again in our hand. And other money have we brought down in our hands to buy food: we cannot tell who put our money in our sacks."

"And he said, Peace be to you, fear not: your God, and the God of your father, hath given you treasure in your sacks: I had your money. And he brought Simeon out unto them. And the man brought the men into Joseph's house, and gave them water, and they washed their feet; and he gave their asses provender. And they made ready the present against Joseph came at noon: for they heard that they should eat bread there."[211]

Joseph's brothers bow down to the earth or make obesience to him as he had dreamed many years ago that they would. They still did not recognize him. Joseph was delighted to see Benjamin. He inquired of their father Israel, and asked if he were alive and well. They informed Joseph father Israel was alive and well. A feast was prepared. The brothers were astonished as Joseph seated them in order of their birth. They were served a sumptious meal. Benjamin's portion was five times as any of the rest. They drank and were merry with him.

(From Genesis) "And when Joseph came home, they brought him the present which was in their hand in the house, and bowed themselves to him to the earth. And he asked them of their welfare, and said, Is your father well, the old man of whom ye spake? Is he yet alive? And they answered, Thy servant our father is in good health, he is yet alive. And they bowed down their heads, and made obeisance. And he lifted up his eyes, and saw his brother Benjamin, his mother's son, and said, Is this your younger brother, of whom ye spake unto me? And he said, God be gracious unto thee, my son."

"And Joseph made haste; for his bowels did yearn upon his brother: and he sought where to weep; and he entered into his chamber, and wept there. And he washed his face, and went out, and refrained himself, and said, Set on bread. And they set on for him by himself, and for them by themselves, and for the Egyptians, which did eat with him, by themselves: because the Egyptians might not eat bread with the Hebrews; for that is an abomination unto the Egyptians."

"And they sat before him, the first born according to his birthright, and the youngest according to his youth: And the men marvelled one at another. And he took and sent messes unto them from before him: but Benjamin's mess was five times so much any of theirs. And they drank, and were merry with him."[212]

Note that Simeon, the brother whom Joseph had retained as surety for these fourteen months, took his place at the feast in order of his birth. Jasher reports that Joseph read the letter from his father Israel and recognized his handwriting. He went to an inner room and wept. When he saw Benjamin the son of his mother Rachel, he again wished to weep, and entered a chamber and wept there. He then washed his face and ordered food to be set on the table. The cup out of which Joseph drank was made of silver, beautifully inlade with onyx stones and bdellium.

Joseph tapped the bottom of the cup on the table to get the attention of his brothers. He pretended the cup had special qualities by which he could divine the order of his brother's birth. Not only were they seated according to the order of their births, but were grouped according to their mothers: Reuben, Simeon, Levi, Judah, Issachar and Zebulum the children of Leah were seated according to their births. And he also placed the others according to their births. Because Benjamin had no available brother to sit with, he was invited to sit with Joseph. During their conversation Joseph asked Benjamin about his family and Benjamin told him about Israel's ten children.

During this conversation Joseph reportedly revealed himself to Benjamin and with him his plan to prove whether his brothers had repented of what they had done to him. Benjamin promised not to tell his brothers of the plan, but apparently knew they would be compelled to return after starting on their journey back to Canaan.[213]

The sacks were again filled with corn. The silver cup was put in Benjamin's sack by Joseph's men. Each brother's money was also returned again to his sack. The journey back to Canaan was begun. The brothers were overtaken, the planted cup was found and the brothers were returned to Egypt to account for their alleged misdeeds.

(From Genesis) "And he commanded the steward of his house, saying, Fill the men's sacks with food, as much as they can carry, and put every man's money in the sacks mouth. And put my cup, the silver cup, in the sack's mouth of the youngest, and his corn's money. And he did according to the word that Joseph had spoken."

"As soon as the morning was light, the men were sent away, they and their asses. And when they were gone out of the city, and not yet far off, Joseph said unto his steward, up, follow after the men; and when thou dost overtake them, say unto them, wherefore have ye rewarded evil for good. Is not this it in which my lord drinketh, and whereby indeed he divineth? ye have done evil in so doing."

"And he overtook them, and he spake unto them these same words. And they said unto him, wherefore saith my lord these words? God forbid that thy servants should do according o this thing: Behold the money, which we found in our sack's mouths, we brought again unto thee out of the land of Canaan: how then should we steal out of thy lord's house silver and gold? With whomsoever of thy servants it be found, both let him die, and we also will be my lord's bondmen. And he said, now also let it be according unto your words: he with whom it is found shall be my servant; and ye shall be blameless."

"Then they speedily took down every man's sack to the ground, and opened every man his sack. And he searched and began at the eldest, and left at the youngest: and the cup was found in Benjamin's sack. Then they rent their clothes and laded every man his ass, and returned to the city."[214]

Not only did they tear their garments, but reportedly they were so angry with Benjamin, thinking he had stolen the cup, that they smote him continually as they were forced to return to the house of Joseph. Judah's anger was kindled and he threatened to destroy all Egypt. Joseph reportedly seized Benjamin, took him into the house and locked the door. Judah broke down the door and a heated exchange of words resulted. Judah boasted of his strength and of his forebears. Again it was Manasseh who somehow quieted and subdued Judah. When he calmed down, Judah was able to convey his true feelings. He would rather take Benjamin's place and let Benjamin be returned to father Israel.[215]

(From Genesis) "And Judah and his brethren came to Joseph's house; for he was yet there: and they fell before him on the ground. And Joseph said unto them, what deed is this that ye have done? wot ye not that such a man as I can certainly divine? And Judah said, what shall we say unto my lord? what shall we speak? or how shall we clear ourselves? God hath found out the iniquity of thy servants: behold, we are my lord's servants, both we, and he also with whom the cup is found. And he said, God forbid that I should do so: but the man in whose hand the cup is found, he shall be my servant; and as for you, get you up in peace unto your father."

"Then Judah came near unto him, and said, O my lord, let thy servant, I pray thee, speak a word in my lord's ears, and let not thine anger burn against thy servant: for thou art even as Pharaoh. My lord asked his servants, saying, Have ye a father, or a brother? And we said unto my lord, We have a father, an old man, and a child of his old age, a little one: and his brother is dead, and he alone is left of his mother, and his father loveth him. And thou saidst unto thy servants, Bring him down unto me, that I may set mine eyes upon him. And we said unto my lord, The lad cannot leave his father: for if he should leave his father, his father would die. And thou saidst unto thy servants, Except your youngest brother come down with you, ye shall see my face no more."

"And it came to pass when we came up unto thy servant my father, we told him the words of my lord. And our father said, Go again, and buy us a little food. And we said, We cannot go down: if our youngest brother be with us, then will we go down: for we may not see the man's face, except our youngest brother be with us. And thy servant my father said unto us, ye know that my wife bare me two sons: And the one went out from me, and I said, Surely he is torn in pieces; and I saw him not since: And if ye take this also from me, and mischief befall him, ye shall bring down my gray hairs with sorrow to the grave."

"Now therefore when I come to thy servant my father, and the lad be not with us; seeing that his life is bound up in the lad's life; It shall come to pass, when he seeth that the lad is not with us, that he will die: and thy servants shall bring down the gray hairs of thy servant our father with sorrow to the grave. For thy servant became surety for the lad unto my father, Saying, If I bring him not unto thee, then I shall bear the blame to my father forever. Now therefore, I pray thee, let thy servant abide instead of the lad a bondman to my lord: and let the lad go up with his brethren. For how shall I go up to my father, and the lad be not with me? lest peradventure I see the evil that shall come on my father."[216]

---

206. Genesis 43:11-14 KJV, MT, JST
207. Jasher LII:26-27; Legends II:91-92
208. Legends II:91-92
209. Ibid II p. 93
210. Genesis 43:15 KJV, MT, JST
211. Ibid 43:16-25
212. Ibid 43:26-34
213. Jasher LIII:1-22 see also Legends II:95-98
214. Genesis 44:1-13
215. Jasher LIII:23-32, LIV:1-67 see also Legends II:103-110
216. Genesis 44:14-34 KJV, MT, JST

CHAPTER XIV

AND GOD SENT ME BEFORE YOU TO PRESERVE YOU A POSTERITY IN THE EARTH AND TO SAVE YOUR LIVES BY A GREAT DELIVERANCE

Judah's willingness to serve as a bondman or slave in exchange for Benjamin's freedom and the happiness that would give Israel (Jacob) touched Joseph. He could not restrain himself any longer before them. He sent out the servants and while alone with the sons of Israel announced he was one of them, their brother, also son of Israel.

(From Genesis) "Then Joseph could not refrain himself before all of them that stood by him: and he cried, Cause every man to go out from me. And there stood no man with him, while Joseph made himself known to his brothers. And he wept aloud: and the Egyptians and the house of Pharaoh heard. And Joseph said unto his brethren, I am Joseph: doth my father yet live? And his brethren could not answer him; for they were troubled at his presence. And Joseph said unto his brethren, Come near to me, I pray you. And they came near. And he said, I am Joseph your brother, whom ye sold into Egypt. Now therefore be not grieved, nor angry with yourselves, that ye sold me hither: for God did send me before you to preserve life."[217]

His brothers were afraid, but Joseph assured them all was forgiven, and announced that he believed it was in the Lord's plan that they sold him, "for God did send me before you to preserve life."[218] In the words of Jasher:

"I am Joseph whom you sold to Egypt, now therefore let it not grieve you that you sold me, for as a support during the famine did God send me before you."[219]

Back to Genesis:

"And God sent me before you to preserve you a posterity in the earth, and to save your lives by a great deliverance. So now it was not you that sent me hither, but God: and he hath made me a father to Pharaoh, and lord of all his house, and a ruler throughout all the land of Egypt. Haste ye, and go up to my father and say unto him, Thus saith thy son Joseph, God hath made me lord of all Egypt: come down unto me, tarry not: And thou shalt dwell in the land of Goshen, and thou shalt be near unto me, thou and thy children, and thy children's children, and thy flocks, and thy herds, and all that thou hast:....And ye shall tell my father of all my glory in Egypt, and of all that ye have seen: and ye shall haste and bring down my father hither."[220]

"And he fell upon his brother Benjamin's neck, and wept; and Benjamin wept upon his neck. Moreover, he kissed all his brethren, and wept upon them: and after that his brethren talked with him."[221]

The Pharaoh agreed to allow Israel and all his family to come to Egypt. Wagon loads of gifts were sent to Jacob (Israel) by Joseph who stayed in Egypt.

(From Genesis) "And the fame thereof was heard in Pharaoh's house, saying, Joseph's brethren are come: and it pleased Pharaoh well, and his servants. And Pharaoh said unto Joseph, Say unto thy brethren, This do ye; lade your beasts, and go, get you unto the land of Canaan; And take your father and your households, and come unto me: and I will give you the good of the land of Egypt, and ye shall eat the fat of the land. Now thou art commanded, this do ye; take you wagons out of the land of Egypt for your little ones, and for your wives, and bring your father, and come. Also regard not your stuff; for the good of all the land of Egypt is yours. And the children of Israel did so: and Joseph gave them wagons, according to the commandment of Pharaoh, and gave them provision for the way."

"To all of them he gave each man changes of raiment;but to Benjamin he gave three hundred pieces of silver, and five changes of raiment. And to his father he sent after this manner; ten asses laden with the good things of Egypt, and ten she asses laden with corn and bread and meat for his father by the way. So he sent his brethren away, and they departed: and he said unto them, See that ye fall not out by the way. And they went up out of Egypt, and came into the land of Canaan unto Jacob their father."²²²

The sons of Israel gently broke the news that Joseph was yet alive, with song and harp by way of Serach the daughter of Asher.

(From Jasher) "And Joseph ceased to command them, and he turned and went back to Egypt, and the sons of Jacob went to the land of Canaan with joy and cheerfulness to their father Jacob. And they came unto the borders of the land, and they said to each other, What shall we do in this matter before our father, for if we come suddenly to him and tell him the matter, he will be greatly alarmed at our words and will not believe us. And they went along until they came nigh unto their houses, and they found Serach, the daughter of Asher, going forth to meet them, and the damsel was very good and subtle, and knew how to play upon the harp. And they called unto her and she came before them, and she kissed them, and they took her and gave unto her a harp, saying, Go now before our father, and sit before him, and strike upon the harp, and speak these words. And they commanded her to go to their house, and she took the harp and hastened before them, and she came and sat near Jacob. And she played well and sang, and uttered in the sweetness of her words, Joseph my uncle is living, and he ruleth throughout the land of Egypt, and is not dead. And she continued to repeat and utter these words, and Jacob heard her words and they were agreeable to him. He listened whilst she repeated them twice and thrice, and joy entered the heart of Jacob at the sweetness of her words, and the spirit of God was upon him, and he knew all her words to be true. And Jacob blessed Serach when she spoke these words before him, and he said unto her, My daughter, may death never prevail over thee, for thou hast revived my spirit; only speak yet before me as thou hast spoken, for thou hast gladdened me with all thy words."

"And she continued to sing these words, and Jacob listened and it pleased him, and he rejoiced, and the spirit of God was upon him. Whilst he was yet speaking with her, behold his sons came to him with horses and chariots and royal garments and servants running before them. And Jacob rose up to meet them, and saw his sons dressed in royal garments and he saw all the treasures that Joseph had sent to them. And they said unto him, Be informed that our brother Joseph is living, and it is he who ruleth throughout the land of Egypt, and it is he who spoke unto us as we told thee. And Jacob heard all the words of his sons, and his heart palpitated at their words, for he could not believe them until he saw all that Joseph had given them and what he had sent him, and all the signs which Joseph had spoken unto them. And they opened out before him, and showed him all that Joseph had sent, they gave unto each what Joseph had sent him, and he knew that they had spoken the truth, and he rejoiced exceedingly on account of his son. And Jacob said, It is enough for me that my son Joseph is still living, I will go and see him before I die."[223]

The Genesis account reads:

"And told him saying, Joseph is yet alive, and he is governor over all the land of Egypt, And Jacob's heart fainted, for he believed them not. And they told him all the words of Joseph, which he had said unto them: and when he saw the wagons which Joseph had sent to carry him, the spirit of Jacob their father revived: And Israel said, It is enough; Joseph my son is yet alive: I will go and see him before I die."[224]

The land of Canaan was promised to Abraham, to Isaac, and to Israel and his posterity as an everlasting inheritance. Israel was understandably reluctant to leave it permanently. Instead he thought he would go to Egypt and visit Joseph, and then return to Canaan. The Lord had other plans for Israel and his family, however, as Israel found out when he came to Beersheba and offered sacrifices where Isaac and Abraham had previously offered them.

Before departing, however, Jacob (Israel) rose up and put on the garments Joseph had sent him. He washed, shaved his hair and put on a turban Joseph had also sent him. His family donned the gifts they had received from him and they rejoiced for three days in the news that Joseph was alive.[225]

The family of Israel departed Canaan for Egypt to visit Joseph. Enroute they stopped at Beersheba and offered sacrifices unto the God of his father Isaac.

(From Genesis) "And Israel took his journey with all that he had, and came to Beersheba, and offered sacrifices unto the God of his father Isaac. And God spake unto Israel in the visions of the night, and said,

Jacob, Jacob, and he said, Here am I. And he said, I am God, the God of thy father; fear not to go down into Egypt; for I will there make of thee a great nation: I will go down with thee into Egypt; and I will also surely bring thee up again; and Joseph shall put his hand upon thine eyes."226

Israel thusly received assurance that it was the Lord's will he move his entire family to Egypt and there become a great nation, there would Israel die, and there would Joseph close Israel's eyes. The Lord God of Israel did indeed make a great nation of him during the next 215 years.* Israel came into Egypt with three score and six (66) souls, and departed with more than 600,000 men of Israel not counting children.227

---

217. Genesis 45:1-5 KJV, MT, JST
218. Genesis 45:5 KJV, MT, JST
219. Jasher LIV:69; Legends II:112
220. Genesis 45:7-13 KJV, MT, JST
221. Genesis 45:14-15 KJV, MT, JST
222. Ibid 45:16-25 KJV, MT, JST
223. Jasher LIV:90-105; Legends II:115-116; V, Yashar wa Yiggash 110a
224. Genesis 45:26-28 KJV, MT, JST
225. Jasher LIV:107-110; Legends II:117; V, Yashar wa-Yiggash, 110a
226. Genesis 46:1-4 KJV, MT, JST
227. Exodus 12:37 KJV, MT, JST

*Antiquities

Chapter XV

AND ISRAEL SAID UNTO JOSEPH, NOW LET ME DIE, SINCE I HAVE SEEN THY FACE, BECAUSE THOU ART YET ALIVE

Israel informed his family and their households that they should go to Egypt for the Lord had thus commanded them. ..."and Jacob rose up with his sons and all his household, and he went out from the land of Canaan from Beersheba with joy and gladness of heart, as they went to the land of Egypt."[228]

Genesis reads:

"And Jacob rose up from Beersheba: and the sons of Israel carried Jacob their father, and their little ones, and their wives, in the wagons which Pharaoh had sent to carry him. And they took their cattle, and their goods, which they had gotten in the land of Canaan, and came into Egypt, Jacob, and all his seed with him: His sons, and his sons' sons with him, his daughters, and his sons' daughters, and all his seed brought he with him into Egypt. And these are the names of the children of Israel, which came into Egypt, Jacob and his sons: Reuben, Jacob's firstborn. And the sons of Reuben; Hanoch, and Phallu, and Hezron, and Carmi. And the sons of Simeon; Jemuel, and Jamin, and Ohad, and Jachin, and Zohar, and Shaul the son of a Canaanitish woman. And the sons of Levi; Gershon, Kohath, and Merari. And the sons of Judah; Er, and Onan, and Shelah, and Pharez, and Zerah: but Er and Onan died in the land of Canaan. And the sons of Pharez were Hezron and Hamul. And the sons of Issachar; Tola, and Phuvah, and Job and Shimron. And the sons of Zebulun; Sered, and Elon, and Jahleel. These be the sons of Leah, which she bare unto Jacob in Padanaram, with his daughter Dinah: all the souls of his sons and his daughters were thirty and three."

"And the sons of Gad; Ziphion, and Haggi, Shuni, and Ezbon, Eri, and Arodi, and Areli. And the sons of Asher; Jimnah, and Ishuah, and Isui, and Beriah, and Serah their sister; and the sons of Beriah; Heber, and Malchiel. These are the sons of Zilpah, whom Laban gave to Leah his daughter, and these she bare unto Jacob, even sixteen souls.

The sons of Rachel Jacob's wife: Joseph, and Benjamin. And unto Joseph in the land of Egypt were born Manasseh and Ephraim, which Asenath the daughter of Poti-pherah priest of On bare unto him. And the sons of Benjamin were Belah, and Becher, and Ashbel, Gera, and Naaman, Ehi, and Rosh, Muppim, and Huppim, and Ard. These are the sons of Rachel, which were born to Jacob: all the souls were fourteen."

"And the sons of Dan; Hushim. And the sons of Naphtali; Jahzeel, and Guni, and Jezer, and Shillem. These are the sons of Bilhah, which Laban gave unto Rachel his daughter, and she bare these unto Jacob: all the souls were seven. All the souls that came with Jacob into Egypt, which came out of his loins, besides Jacob's sons' wives, all the souls were threescore and six."[229]

Israel sent Judah in advance of the family of sixty-six. He met Joseph and received instructions to settle in Goshen in the land of Egypt, where Joseph and the Pharaoh had assigned them. Judah returned to his father and family and led them there.

(From Genesis) "And he sent Judah before him unto Joseph, to direct his face unto Goshen; and they came into the land of Goshen. And Joseph made ready his chariot, and went up to meet Israel his father, to Goshen, and presented himself unto him, and he fell on his neck, and wept on his neck a good while."[230]

Jasher amplified the reunion:

"And Joseph harnessed the chariot and he assembled all his mighty men and his servants and all the officers of Egypt in order to go and meet his father Jacob, and Joseph's mandate was proclaimed in Egypt, saying, All that do not go to meet Jacob shall die. And on the next day Joseph went forth with all Egypt a great and mighty host, all dressed in garments of fine linen, and purple and with instruments of silver and gold and with instruments of war with them."

"And they all went to meet Jacob with all sorts of musical instruments, with drums and timbrels, strewing myrrh and aloes all along the road, and they all went after this fashion, and the earth shook at their shouting. And all the women of Egypt went upon the roofs of Egypt and upon the walls to meet Jacob, and upon the head of Joseph was Pharaoh's regal crown, for Pharaoh had sent it unto him to put on at the time of his going to meet his father."

"And when Joseph came within fifty cubits of his father, he alighted from the chariot and he walked toward his father and when all the officers of Egypt and her nobles saw that Joseph had gone on foot toward his father, they also alighted and walked on foot toward Jacob. And when Jacob approached the camp of Joseph, Jacob observed the camp that was coming toward him with Joseph, and it gratified him and Jacob was astonished at it."

"And Jacob said unto Judah, Who is that man whom I see in the camp of Egypt dressed in kingly robes with a very red garment upon him and a royal crown upon his head, who has alighted from his chariot and is coming toward us? and Judah answered his father saying, He is thy son Joseph the king; and Jacob rejoiced in seeing the glory of his son."

"And Joseph came nigh unto his father and bowed to his father, and all the men of the camp bowed to the ground with him before Jacob. And behold Jacob ran and hastened to his son Joseph and fell upon his neck and kissed him, and they wept, and Joseph also embraced his father and kissed him, and they wept and all the people of Egypt wept with them."[231]

Returning to Genesis:

"And Israel said unto Joseph, Now let me die, since I have seen thy face, because thou art yet alive."[232]

And Jasher's description:

"And Jacob said unto Joseph, Now I will die cheerfully after I have seen thy face, that thou art still living and with glory.[233]

The rest of Joseph's family also greet him:

> "And the sons of Jacob and their wives and children and their servants, and all the household of Jacob wept exceedingly with Joseph, and they kissed him and wept greatly with him."[234]

Joseph took leave of Israel, returned and reported to the Pharaoh the arrival of Israel and his family in Goshen. Joseph arranged for some of his brethren to meet the Pharaoh in advance of Israel, including Reuben, Issachar, Zebulun, and Benjamin.

> (From Genesis) "and Pharaoh said unto his brethren, What is your occupation? And they said unto Pharaoh, Thy servants are shepherds, both we, and also our fathers. They said moreover unto Pharaoh, For to sojourn in the land are we come; for thy servants have no pasture for their flocks; for the famine is sore in the land of Canaan: now therefore, we pray thee, let thy servants dwell in the land of Goshen. And Pharaoh spake unto Joseph, saying, Thy father and thy brethren are come unto thee: The land of Egypt is before thee; in the best of the land make thy father and brethren to dwell; in the land of Goshen let them dwell: and if thou knowest any men of activity among them, then make them rulers over my cattle."[235]

Shepherds were an abomination to the Egyptians. By identifying themselves as such made it easier for Joseph to settle Israel in Goshen, apart from the Egyptians. The Pharaoh agreed, and the sons of Israel took leave.

Afterwards, Joseph brought Jacob to visit with the Pharaoh. The Pharaoh was blessed by Jacob (Israel). The Pharaoh enquired as to Jacob's age; and he answered, one hundred thirty years, adding that he hasn't lived as long as his fathers (Isaac, Abraham, Eber, Shem) had lived.

Genesis states:

> "And Joseph brought in Jacob his father, and set him before Pharaoh: and Jacob blessed Pharaoh. And Pharaoh said unto Jacob, How

old art thou? And Jacob said unto Pharaoh, The days of the years of my pilgrimage are an hundred and thirty years: few and evil have the days of the years of my life been, and have not attained unto the days of the years of the life of my fathers in the days of their pilgrimage. And Jacob blessed Pharaoh, and went out from before Pharaoh."[236]

---

228. Jasher LV:5; Legends II:118-119; V, Yashar Wa-Yiggash, 110a - 110b
229. Genesis 46:5-27 KJV, MT, JST 230. Ibid 46:28-29 KJV, MT, JST
231. Jasher LV:7-15; Legends II:120-121; V, Yashar Wa-Yiggash 110b - 111a
232. Genesis 46:30 KJV, MT, JST
233. Jasher LV:16; Legends II:122; V, Yashar Wa-Yiggash 110b - 111a
234. Ibid LV:17
235. Genesis 47:3-6 KJV, MT, JST
236. Ibid 47:7-10

Chapter XVI

THOU SHALT CARRY ME OUT OF EGYPT

(From Genesis) "And Joseph placed his father and his brethren, and gave them a possession in the land of Egypt, in the best of the land, in the land of Rameses, as Pharaoh had commanded. And Joseph nourished his father, and his brethren, and all his father's household, with bread, according to their families."[237]

To which Jasher adds:

"And Joseph gave unto them the best part of the whole land; the best of Egypt had they all the days of Joseph; and Joseph also gave unto them and unto the whole of his father's household, clothes and garments year by year; and the sons of Jacob remained securely in Egypt all the days of their brother. And Jacob always ate at Joseph's table, Jacob and his sons did not leave Joseph's table day or night, besides what Jacob's children consumed in their houses...."

"And Jacob and his sons dwelt in the land of Egypt in the land of Goshen, and they took possession in it, and they were fruitful and multiplied in it."[238]

During the first five years of Israel's sojourn in Egypt the famine worsened. Joseph continued to parcel out the remaining food in the storehouses, selling it for whatever means of exchange was available, money until it ran out, silver and gold, horses and flocks and cattle, then the land he bought for Pharaoh.

Jasher and the Legends indicate that Joseph took the silver and gold collected, and buried it. Some of it he buried near the Red Sea, some by the river Perath, some he gave to his brothers, and some he gave to the Pharaoh.

The seven years of famine came to an end. Seeds were given out and allowed to be planted. A fifth of the crop was to be given to the Pharaoh and four fifths retained unto themselves. Conditions returned to normal after the famine abated and there was sufficient food.

Except to report that "Israel dwelt in the land of Egypt, in the country of Goshen; and they had possessions therein, and grew, and multiplied exceedingly,"[239] nothing more is said of Israel's final seventeen years, until he approached death.

As the end of Israel's life nears much of significance transpires.

He obtained a promise from his sons that they would bury him in Machpelah in Hebron with his father Isaac and grandfather Abraham. He blessed all of his sons and some of his grandsons including Ephraim and Manasseh. Jasher and the Legends report that Israel prophesied the Lord would raise up a servant (Moses) among them who would deliver them from affliction and bring them back to the land of their fathers.

Jasher and the Legends also report that Israel identified those who were to carry his bier at his death. Joseph wasn't to help carry it, for he was a king. Levi was not to help carry Israel's bier either. Instead, he and his sons were to carry the Ark of the Covenant. Note that this is a reference to the Ark of the Covenant in Israel's day. It was Levi's posterity of the priesthood through Moses and Aaron who took care of the Ark of the Covenant and carried it, in their day and thereafter. Was this a prophesy of what was to come, or did the Ark of the Covenant exist in Israel's and Levi's day?

And now for the actual report.

(From Genesis) "And Jacob lived in the land of Egypt seventeen years: so the whole age of Jacob was an hundred forty and seven years. And the time drew nigh that Israel must die: and he called his son Joseph, and said unto him, If now I have found grace in thy sight, put, I pray thee, thy hand under my thigh, and deal kindly and truly with me; bury me not, I pray thee, in Egypt: But I will lie with my fathers, and thou shalt carry me out of Egypt, and bury me in their buryingplace. And he said, I will do as thou hast said. And he said, Swear unto me, And he sware unto him. And Israel bowed himself upon the bed's head."[240]

From the Legends:

"Carry me out of the land of idolatry and bury me in the land where God hath caused His name to dwell...."[241]

And from Jasher:

"And Jacob lived in the land of Egypt seventeen years, and the days of Jacob, and the years of his life were a hundred and forty seven years. At that time Jacob was attacked with that illness of which he died and he sent and called for his son Joseph from Egypt, and Joseph his son came from Egypt and Joseph came unto his father. And Jacob said unto Joseph and unto his sons, Behold I die, and the God of our ancestors will visit you, and bring you back to the land, which the Lord sware to give unto you and unto your children after you, now therefore when I am dead, bury me in the cave which is in Machpelah in Hebron in the land of Canaan, near my ancestors. And Jacob made his sons swear to bury him in Machpelah, in Hebron, and his sons swore unto him concerning this thing.[242]

Knowing, therefore, his posterity would be brought back out of Egypt in the future, Israel sought to be buried in the land of his inheritance promised to Abraham, Isaac and himself and their posterity.

During this visit with Joseph, Israel bore testimony of the Lord God's appearance unto him in Luz (Bethel) and of the blessings God promised him there, before he was married and had children. God Almighty had promised Israel he would make of him a multitude of people and give his posterity an everlasting possession.

Genesis reads:

"And it came to pass after these things, that one told Joseph, Behold, thy father is sick: and he took with him his two sons, Manasseh and Ephraim. And one told Jacob, and said, Behold, thy son Joseph cometh unto thee: and Israel strengthened himself, and sat upon the bed. And Jacob said unto Joseph, God Almighty appeared unto me at Luz in the land of Canaan, and blessed me. And said unto me, Behold, I will make thee fruitful, and multiply thee, and I will make of thee a multitude of people; and will give this land to thy seed after thee for an everlasting possession."[243]

The Legends:

"The Holy spirit made known to Jacob that Joseph was coming to him....He strengthened himself spiritually as well as physically, by prayer to God, in which he besought Him to let the holy spirit descend upon him at the time of his giving the blessings to the sons of Joseph."[244]

After testifying to Joseph of his experience and blessings in Luz (Bethel) years ago, Israel blessed his son Joseph and his grandsons Ephraim and Manasseh born through Rachel, whom he had buried near Ephrath (Bethlehem) years before. Israel prophecied concerning Joseph, blessed these two grandsons and made them equal by inheritance with his own sons. Israel also testified that God shall be with Joseph, and bring his posterity up to the land of his fathers, where Joseph's posterity would have one portion above his brethren.

Genesis reads:

"And now thy two sons, Ephraim and Manasseh, which were born unto thee in the land of Egypt, before I came unto thee into Egypt, are mine; as Reuben and Simeon, they shall be mine. And thy issue, which thou begettest after them, shall be thine, and shall be called after the name of their brethren in their inheritance."[245]

To which JST Genesis adds:

"And now, of thy two sons, Ephraim and Manasseh, which were born unto thee in the land of Egypt, before I came unto thee into Egypt; behold they are mine, and the God of my fathers shall bless them; even as Reuben and Simeon they shall be blessed, for they are mine; wherefore they shall be called after my name. (Therefore they were called Israel)."

"And thy issue which thou begettest after them, shall be thine, and shall be called after the name of their brethren in their inheritance, in the tribes; therefore they were called the tribes of Manasseh and Ephraim. And Jacob said unto Joseph when the God of my fathers appeared unto me in Luz, in the land of Canaan; he sware unto me, that he would give unto me, and unto my seed, the land for an everlasting possession. Therefore, O my son, he hath blessed me in raising thee up to be a servant unto me, in saving my house from death; In delivering my people, thy brethren, from famine which was sore in the land; wherefore the God of thy fathers shall bless thee, and the fruit of thy loins, that they shall be blessed above thy brethren, and above thy father's house;"

"For thou hast prevailed, and thy father's house hast bowed down unto thee, even as it was shown unto thee, before thou wast sold into Egypt by the hands of thy brethren; wherefore thy brethren shall bow down unto thee, from generation to generation, unto the fruit of thy loins forever; For thou shalt be a light unto my people to deliver them in the days of their captivity, from bondage; and to bring salvation unto them, when they are altogether bowed down under sin."[246]

The seed of Joseph then, was/is to bring salvation unto the house of Israel some time in the future when the house of Israel is bowed down under sin.

Returning to KJV Genesis:

"And as for me, when I came from Padan, Rachel died by me in the land of Canaan in the way, when yet there was but a little way to come unto Ephrath: and I buried her there in the way of Ephrath; the same is Bethlehem. And Israel beheld Joseph's sons, and said, Who are these? And Joseph said unto his father, They are my sons, whom God hath given me in this place. And he said, Bring them, I pray thee, unto me, and I will bless them. Now the eyes of Israel were dim for age, so that he could not see. And he brought them near unto him; and he kissed them, and embraced them. And Israel said unto Joseph, I had not thought to see thy face: and, lo, God hath shewed me also thy seed. And Joseph brought them out from between his knees, and he bowed himself with his face to the earth. And Joseph took them both, Ephraim in his right hand toward Israel's left hand, and Manasseh in his left hand toward Israel's right hand, and brought them near unto him. And Israel stretched out his right hand, and laid it upon Ephraim's head, who was the younger, and his left hand upon Manasseh's head, guiding his hands wittingly; for Manasseh was the firstborn. And he blessed Joseph, and said, God, before whom my fathers Abraham and Isaac did walk, the God which fed me all my life long unto this day. The Angel which redeemed me from all evil, bless the lads; and let my name be named on them, and the name of my fathers Abraham and Isaac; and let them grow in to a multitude in the midst of the earth."

Continuing:

"And when Joseph saw that his father laid his right hand upon the head of Ephraim, it displeased him: and he held up his father's hand, to remove it from Ephraim's head unto Manasseh's head. And Joseph said unto his father, Not so, my father: for this is the firstborn; put thy right hand upon his head. And his father refused, and said, I know it, my son, I know it: he also shall become a people, and he also shall be great: but truly his younger brother shall be greater than he, and his seed shall become a multitude of nations. And he blessed them that day, saying, In thee shall Israel bless, saying, God make thee as Ephraim and as Manasseh: and he set Ephraim before Manasseh. And Israel said unto Joseph, Behold, I die: but God shall be with you, and bring you again unto the land of your fathers. Moreover I have given to thee one portion above thy brethren, which I took out of the hand of the Amorite with my sword and with my bow."[247]

From these verses we learn that Ephraim received the greater blessing and responsibility, that his seed was to become a multitude of nations, and that Israel anticipated God would bring his posterity out of Egypt back to Canaan, the land of their inheritance, in the future.

The Legends add that Ephraim was receiving instruction in the Torah (Law of the Gospel) from Jacob and that he was one of those who notified Joseph of Jacob's illness. They also report Ephraim's special blessing from his grandfather Jacob as follows:

"Ephraim, my son, thou art the head of the academy, and in the days to come my most excellent and celebrated descendants will be called Ephrati after thee."[248]

Israel brought his interview with Joseph, Ephraim, and Manasseh to a close and requested that all of his sons and their children be gathered together so that he could bless them also.

The first day with all his children and grandchildren in general assembly sitting before him, Israel blessed them and declared to them:

(From Jasher)..."Serve the Lord your God, for he who delivered your fathers will also deliver you from all trouble....The Lord God of your fathers shall grant you a thousand times as much and bless you, and may he give you the blessing of your father Abraham; and all the children of Jacob's sons went forth on that day after he had blessed them."

...."and on the next day Jacob again called for his sons, and they all assembled and came to him and sat before him, and Jacob on that day blessed his sons before his death, each man did he bless according to his blessing; behold it is written in the book of the law of the Lord appertaining to Israel."[249]

Genesis reads:

"And Jacob called unto his sons, and said, Gather yourselves together, that I may tell you that which shall befall you in the last days. Gather yourselves together and hear ye sons of Jacob; and hearken unto Israel your father."[250]

Back to Jasher:

"And Jacob again commanded his sons on that day, saying, Behold I shall be this day gathered unto my people; carry me up from Egypt, and bury me in the cave of Machpelah as I have commanded you. Howbeit take heed I pray you that none of your sons carry me, only yourselves, and this is the manner you shall do unto me, when you carry my body to go with it to the land of Canaan to bury me, Judah, Issachar and Zebulun shall carry my bier at the eastern side; Reuben, Simeon and Gad at the south, Ephraim, Manasseh and Benjamin at the west, Dan, Asher and Naphtali at the north. Let not Levi carry with you, for he and his sons will carry the Ark of the Covenant of the Lord with the Israelites in the camp, neither let Joseph my son carry, for as a king so let his glory be; howbeit, Ephraim and Manasseh shall be in their stead. Thus shall you do unto me when you carry me away; do not neglect anything of all that I command you; and it shall come to pass when you do this unto me, that the Lord will remember you favorably and your children after you forever."

Continuing:

"and you my sons, honor each his brother and his relative, and command your children and your children's children after you to serve the Lord God of your ancestors all the days. In order that you may prolong your days in the land, you and your children and your children's children for ever, when you do what is good and upright in the sight of the Lord your God, to go in all his ways. And thou, Joseph my son, forgive I pray thee the wrongs of thy brethren and all their misdeeds in the injury that they heaped upon thee, for God intended it for thine and thy children's benefit. And O my son leave not thy brethren to the inhabitants of Egypt, neither hurt their feelings, for behold I consign them to the hand of God and in thy hand to guard them from the Egyptians; and the sons of Jacob answered their father saying, O, our father, all that thou hast commanded us, so will we do; may God only be with us."

"And Jacob said unto his sons, So may God be with you when you keep all his ways; turn not from his ways either to the right or the left in performing what is good and upright in his sight. For I know that many and grievous troubles will befall you in the latter days in the land, yea your children and children's children, only serve the Lord and he will save you from all trouble. And it shall come to pass when you shall go after God to serve him and will teach your children after you, and your children's children, to know the Lord, then will the Lord raise up unto you and your children a servant from amongst your children, and the Lord will deliver you through his hand from all affliction, and bring you out of Egypt and bring you back to the land of your fathers to inherit it securely."[251]

The Legends:

"According to my power did I bless you, but in future days a prophet will arise, and this man Moses will bless you too, and he will continue my blessings where I left off."[252]

Israel prophesied thus that his posterity would be afflicted and be put in bondage and that God would raise up a servant (Moses) who would deliver them from that bondage.

Using allegories Israel gave each of his twelve sons a blessing and prophesied what would befall them and their posterity in the last days.

To Judah, Israel declared:

....."Thou art he whom thy brethren shall praise: thy hand shall be in the neck of thine enemies; thy father's children shall bow down before thee. Judah is a lion's whelp; from the prey, my son thou art gone up; he stooped down, he couched as a lion, and as an old lion, who shall rouse him up? The sceptre shall not depart from Judah, nor a lawgiver from between his feet, until Shiloh come; and unto him shall the gathering of the people be."

"Binding his foal unto the vine, and his ass's colt unto the choice vine, he washed his garments in wine, and his clothes in the blood of grapes. His eyes shall be red with wine, and his teeth white with milk."253

To which Jasher adds:

"And Jacob said unto Judah, I know my son that thou art a mighty man for thy brethren, reign over them, and thy sons shall reign over their sons forever. Only teach thy sons the bow and all weapons of war, in order that they may fight the battles of their brother who will rule over his enemies."254

And the Legends:

"No people and no kingdom will be able to stand up against thee. Rulers shall not cease from the house of Judah, nor teachers of the law from his posterity, until his descendant Messiah come, and the obedience of all peoples be unto him, How glorious is Messiah of the house of Judah!"255

From Levi were to come the priesthood and the scholars that

would expound the law of the Gospel (Torah) and render decisions according to its teachings. In other words, common judges in Israel were to be appointed among the people from the descendants of Levi, or who held the Levitical Priesthood.[256]

To Joseph, Israel declared:

"Joseph is a fruitful bough, even a fruitful bough by a well; whose branches run over the wall: The archers have sorely grieved him, and shot at him, and hated him: But his bow abode in strength, and the arms of his hands were made strong by the hands of the mighty God of Jacob; (from thence is the shepherd,* the stone of Israel:) Even by the God of thy father, who shall help thee; and by the Almighty, who shall bless thee with blessings of heaven above, blessings of the deep that lieth under, blessings of the breasts, and of the womb: The blessings of thy father have prevailed above the blessings of my progenitors unto the utmost bound of the everlasting hills: they shall be on the head of Joseph, and on the crown of the head of him that was separate from his brethren."[257]

The Legends declare Joseph's blessing as having exceeded the blessing of all his brethren. Jacob spoke:

"O son whom I bred up, Joseph, whom I raised, and who wast strong to resist the enticements of sin, thou didst conquer all the magicians and the wise men of Egypt by thy wisdom....May the blessing of thy father giveth thee now, and the blessing that his father's Abraham and Isaac gave him - may all these blessings be a crown upon the head of Joseph, and....yet diminish(ed) not the honor due his brethren."[258]

The blessings Israel gave to his other sons along with the story of their lives and the lives of Judah and Joseph not already reported are contained in the chapters that follow.

Israel closed his blessings on his twelve sons and charged them again to bury him in the cave of Machpelah in Hebron in the land of Canaan with his parents Isaac and Rebekah and grandparents Abraham and Sarah; and with his wife Leah.

Genesis reads:

"All these are the twelve tribes of Israel: and this is it that their father spake unto them, and blessed them; every one according to his blessing he blessed them. And he charged them, and said unto them, I am to be gathered unto my people: bury me with my fathers in the cave that is in the field of Ephron the Hittite, In the cave that is in the field of Machpelah, which is before Mamre, in the land of Canaan, which Abraham bought with the field of Ephron the Hittite for a possession a buringplace. There they buried Abraham and Sarah his wife; there they buried Isaac and Rebekah his wife; and there I buried Leah. The purchase of the field and of the cave that is therein was from the children of Heth. And when Jacob had made an end of commanding his sons, he gathered up his feet into the bed, and yielded up the ghost (expired), and was gathered unto his people."[259]

---

237. Genesis 47:11-12 KJV, MT, JST
238. Jasher LV:27-28, 36
239. Genesis 47:27; Legends II:128-130
240. Genesis 47:28-31 KJV, MT, JST
241. Legends II:128
242. Jasher LVI:1-4
243. Genesis 48:1-4 KJV, MT, JST
244. Legends II:133
245. Genesis 48:5-6; Legends II:134
246. Genesis 48:5-11 JST
247. Genesis 48:7-22 KJV, MT (48:12-28), JST
248. Legends II:132, 138
249. Jasher LVI:5-7
250. Genesis 49:1-2 KJV, MT, JST
251. Jasher LVI:10-21; Legends II:148; V, Yasher Wa Yehi 112a - 112b
252. Legends II:147
253. Genesis 49:8-12 KJV, MT, JST
254. Jasher LVI:8-9
255. Legends II:143
256. Ibid II:143
257. Genesis 49:22-26 KJV, MT, JST *It is from the lineage of Jacob that the Messiah comes.
258. Legends II:146
259. Genesis 49:28-33 KJV, MT, JST

Chapter XVII

AND JOSEPH WENT UP TO BURY HIS FATHER

The twelve sons of Israel led by Joseph carried out the wishes of their father. After he was embalmed, a great mourning, a seventy day mourning, was held for Israel in Egypt. Following the days of mourning in Egypt, Israel's sons and all their families traveled to Canaan and buried him there in the cave of Machpelah.

Genesis reads:

> "And when Jacob had made an end of commanding his sons, he gathered up his feet into the bed, and yielded up the ghost, and was gathered unto his people."[260]

> "And Joseph fell upon his father's face, and wept upon him, and kissed him. And Joseph commanded his servants the physicians to embalm his father: and the physicians embalmed Israel. And forty days were fulfilled for him; for so are fulfilled the days of those which are embalmed: and the Egyptians mourned for him threescore and ten days. And when the days of his mourning (weeping) were past, Joseph spake unto the house of Pharaoh, saying, If now I have found grace in your eyes, speak, I pray you, in the ears of Pharaoh, saying, My father made me swear, saying, Lo, I die: in my grave which I have digged for me in the land of Canaan, there shalt thou bury me. Now therefore let me go up, I pray thee, and bury my father, and I will come again. And Pharaoh said, Go up, and bury thy father, according as he made thee swear."[261]

Jasher adds:

> "And his sons' wives and all his household came and fell upon Jacob, and they wept over him, and cried in a very loud voice concern-

ing Jacob. And all the sons of Jacob rose up together, and they tore their garments, and they all put sackcloth upon their loins, and they fell upon their faces, and they cast dust upon their heads toward the heavens. And the thing was told unto Osnath Joseph's wife, and she rose up and put on a sack and she with all the Egyptian women with her came and mourned and wept for Jacob. And also all the people of Egypt who knew Jacob came all on that day when they heard this thing, and all Egypt wept for many days. And also from the land of Canaan did the women come unto Egypt when they heard that Jacob was dead, and they wept for him in Egypt for seventy days. And it came to pass after this that Joseph commanded his servants the doctors to embalm his father with myrrh and frankincense and all manner of incense and perfume, and the doctors embalmed Jacob as Joseph had commanded them. And all the people of Egypt and the elders and all the inhabitants of the land of Goshen wept and mourned over Jacob, and all his sons and the children of his household lamented and mourned over their father Jacob many days."

"And after the days of his weeping had passed away, at the end of seventy days, Joseph said unto Pharaoh, I will go up and bury my father in the land of Canaan as he made me swear, and then I will return. And Pharaoh sent Joseph, saying, Go up and bury thy father as he said, and as he made thee swear; and Joseph rose up with all his brethren to go to the land of Canaan to bury their father Jacob as he had commanded them. And Pharaoh commanded that it should be proclaimed throughout Egypt, saying, Whoever goeth not up with Joseph and his brethren to the land of Canaan to bury Jacob, shall die. And all Egypt heard of Pharaoh's proclamation, and they all rose up together, and all the servants of Pharaoh, and the elders of his house, and all the elders of the land of Egypt went up with Joseph, and all the officers and nobles of Pharaoh went up as the servants of Joseph, and they went to bury Jacob in the land of Canaan."[262]

The funeral procession must have stretched for miles for not only did it include the house of Israel, but the servants of Pharaoh and all the elders of the land of Egypt as well.

Genesis reads:

"And Joseph went up to bury his father: and with him went up all the servants of Pharaoh, the elders of his house, and all the elders of the land of Egypt, And all the house of Joseph, and his brethren, and his father's house: only their little ones, and their flocks, and their herds, they left in the land of Goshen. And there went up with him both chariots and horsemen: and it was a very great company."[263]

To which Jasher adds:

"And the sons of Jacob carried the bier upon which he lay; according to all that their father commanded them, so did his sons unto him. And the bier was of pure gold, and it was inlaid round about with onyx stones and bdellium; and the cover of the bier was gold woven work, joined with threads, and over them were hooks of onyx stones and bdellium. And Joseph placed upon the head of his father Jacob a large golden crown, and he put a golden sceptre in his hand, and they surrounded the bier as was the custom of kings during their lives. And all the troops of Egypt went before him in this array, at first all the mighty men of Pharaoh, and the mighty men of Joseph, and after them the rest of the inhabitants of Egypt, and they were all girded with swords and equipped with coats of mail, and the trappings of war were upon them. And all the weepers and mourners went at a distance opposite to the bier, going and weeping and lamenting, and the rest of the people went after the bier. And Joseph and his household went together near the bier barefooted and weeping, and the rest of Joseph's servants went around him; each man had his ornaments upon him, and they were all armed with their weapons of war. And fifty of Jacob's servants went in front of the bier, and they strewed along the road myrrh and aloes, and all manner of perfume, and all the sons of Jacob that carried the bier walked upon the perfumery, and the servants of Jacob went before them strewing the perfume along the road. And Joseph went up with a heavy camp, and they did after this manner every day until they reached the land of Canaan...."[264]

The procession stopped at the threshing floor of Atad in the land of Canaan where they were joined by the Canaanites and together the house of Israel, the Egyptians and the Canaanites mourned for Jacob (Israel) and lamented another seven days.

From Genesis:

"And they came to the threshing floor of Atad, which is beyond Jordan, and there they mourned with a great and very sore lamentation: and he made a mourning for his father seven days. And when the inhabitants of the land, the Canaanites, saw the mourning in the floor of Atad, they said, This is a grievous mourning to the Egyptians: wherefore the name of it was called Abel-mizraim, which is beyond Jordan."[265]

To which Jasher adds:

"....and they came to the threshing floor of Atad, which was on the other side of Jordan, and they mourned an exceeding great and heavy mourning in that place. And all the kings of Canaan heard of this thing and they all went forth, each man from his house, thirty-one kings of Canaan, and they all came with their men to mourn and weep over Jacob. And all these kings beheld Jacob's bier, and behold Joseph's crown was upon it, and they also put their crowns upon the bier, and encircled it with crowns. And all these kings made in that place a great and heavy mourning with the sons of Jacob and Egypt over Jacob, for all the kings of Canaan knew the valor of Jacob and his sons."[266]

Genesis reports that Israel's sons buried him in the cave of Machpelah as he requested and returned to Egypt. The remaining eleven verses of Genesis are devoted to Joseph and his brethren. The Genesis account of Jacob's (Israel's) life ends as follows:

"And his sons did unto him as he commanded them: For his sons carried him into the land of Canaan, and buried him in the cave of the field of Machpelah, which Abraham bought with the field for a possession of a buryingplace of Ephron the Hittite, before Mamre."[267]

Jasher and the Legends, on the other hand, report that as the huge funeral procession neared its destination, Esau received a report saying Jacob, his brother, had died in Egypt, and that his sons and all Egypt were conveying him to the land of Canaan for burial. Esau's wrath was rekindled, he assembled his substantial followers including the sons of Ishmael and Keturah under the pretense they too would mourn for Jacob (Israel). After feign mourning with all those assembled, Esau and his followers blocked the entrance of the cave of

Machpelah as he stood before Joseph, his brethren and all that came with him from Egypt.

Joseph and his brethren inquired of Esau as to why they were blocking the cave. Esau claimed that the cave belonged to him and his fathers (Isaac and Abraham). Joseph responded by saying his father Israel had title to the cave and that the transaction of purchase was back in Egypt. Esau advised that the records be brought to Canaan, and that he Esau would abide by them. Naphtali, Joseph's brother, was swift of foot and he it was that was sent back to Egypt to get the records including those which contained "all the transactions of the birthright which are written, fetch thou."

Naphtali departed for Egypt, and Esau increased his resistance. He began a battle with Joseph and his brethren. Forty of Esau's men were slain.

Chushim, son of Dan, son of Jacob, watched the battle from a hundred cubits distant. Chushim was deaf, understanding only the voice of consternation among them. He inquired "Why do you not bury the dead and what is this consternation?" Chushim then quickly ran into the battle and slew Esau and cut off his head. The loss of Esau disoriented his followers and the sons of Jacob prevailed.[268]

> (From Jasher) "And Jacob was buried in Hebron, in the cave of Machpelah which Abraham had bought from the sons of Heth for the possession of a burial place, and he was buried in very costly garments. And no king had such honor paid him as Joseph paid unto his father at his death, for he buried him with great honor like unto the burial of kings."[269]

So Israel's life came to a close. The mantle of leadership fell upon Joseph whom Israel had anointed and blessed as the leader of the Lord's covenant people. They continued to reside in Egypt at the discretion of the Pharaoh.

It has been written that Israel:

- was chosen for his role on earth before he was born in the flesh
- was accorded the privilege of asking God what he would

- was a priest before God, having the power to act for Him
- wore priestly garments
- was named by the Lord Himself
- gave tithes of his possessions
- received revelations from the Holy Spirit/God
- was a friend, servant and prophet of God
- foretold the future of Israel through his sons
- was a proscelyte/missionary
- loved the Lord God Jehovah with all his heart, offered sacrifices often and had no other Gods before Him
- honored his father and mother

For his efforts Israel was granted his exaltation, and he, Israel also sitteth upon his celestial throne. "And Jacob did none other things than that which (he was commanded, (he had) entered into his exaltation, according to (God's) promises and sit/s upon thrones...."[270]

---

260. Genesis 49:33 KJV, MT, JST
261. Ibid 50:1-6 KJV, MT, JST
262. Jasher LVI:24-34; Legends II:149-151
263. Genesis 50:7-9 KJV, MT, JST
264. Jasher LVI:35-42; Legends II:152-3
265. Genesis 50:10-11 KJV, MT, JST
266. Jasher LVI:42-45; Legends II:153-4
267. Genesis 50:12-13 KJV, MT, JST
268. Jasher LVI:46-65; Legends II:153-54
269. Ibid LVI:66-67
270. Doctrine & Covenants 132:37

Chapter XVIII

FROM THE DEATH OF ISRAEL TO THE DEATH OF LEVI

Israel died in Joseph's fifty sixth year or seventeen years after moving his family to Egypt. The Genesis report of his remaining fifty-four years is covered in thirteen verses of Chapter 50 (14-26). Levi apparently lived to age one hundred thirty seven some twenty two years after Joseph's death. Exodus begins with an enumeration of the twelve sons of Israel, reporting they were all dead. We must turn, therefore, to other sources to cover the final period of the remaining seventy five years of the sons of Israel, ending with Levi who was apparently the last of them to die.

Although in Egypt living in the land of Goshen with many favors and blessings, conflict between the twelve sons of Israel and the sons of Esau continued. Following the death of Esau, the sons of Israel continued to battle with the sons of Esau. Israel's sons prevailed and took captive Zepho, son of Eliphaz, son of Esau, and others. These captives were brought back with them as they returned from burying Israel in the cave of Machpelah in Hebron.

Other sons of Esau, not captured, enlisted the help of Angeas, king of Africa, in their efforts to free Zepho and the other prisoners held by the sons of Israel. The Midianites were also enlisted by them to help set Zepho free. Internal battles developed among the allies of Esau including the people of Seir and the people of Esau who had intermarried with them. To settle these power struggles they sought a king not of their own, but of the people of Laban, who were living in Africa in the City of Dinahah. Bela, son of Beor, was the person selected to be their king, and he reigned thirty years.[271]

The Pharaoh, who had made Joseph his second, died in the thirty second year of the sons of Israel's sojourn in Egypt, or fifteen years after Israel's death. Magron, his son, was appointed to succeed him with some special conditions. Joseph was to serve as father to Magron and Magron was to be under Joseph's care and counsel. Apparently Joseph was held in such high esteem by the people of Egypt, that they consented to this arrangement. Magron was forty one years old when he began to reign. Joseph was seventy one years old. Magron may well have been the son of the Pharaoh, whose birth was prophesied by Joseph, in whom the Pharaoh would take comfort after the death of his first born two year old son.

This arrangement with Magron and Joseph continued thirty nine more years until Joseph's death. Joseph continued to superintend all of Egypt. The people, for the most part, inclined toward Joseph, loved him, and accepted what amounted to Joseph, being the king of Egypt. Some, however, resented him. They preferred one of their own to rule.

During these years Joseph led the armies of Egypt in battles against surrounding enemies including the Philistines. Egypt's jurisdiction and influence was broadened in these battles to include areas bounded by the great river Perath and extended to Canaan and Zidon. Yearly taxes were paid to Joseph who accepted them in behalf of Egypt. Joseph and his brethren dwelt securely in the land of Egypt. They were fruitful and multiplied exceedingly, and they served the Lord God Jehovah as father Israel had commanded them to do.

The children of Esau also were fruitful and multiplied exceedingly, being part of the promise given to Abraham and Isaac, that their posterity would become as numerous as the stars in the sky, and grains of sand of the sea. They were still unable to free Zepho and others from captivity, though they tried. Joseph's armies prevailed each time. Leadership of the children of Esau passed from Bela to Jobab, the son of Zarach, (Zerah) of Botzrah (Bozrah) in the eighty ninth year of Joseph. He was of the children of the east, and may have been of Ishmael, rather than Esau. Jobab reigned ten years and was succeeded by Husham (Chusham) of the land of Temani until Joseph's ninety-ninth year. Husham reigned twenty years and was the leader of the children of Esau when Joseph died.[272] Successors to Husham were Hadad, son of Bedad, Samlah of Masreki, Saul of Rehoboth, Baal-hanan, son of Achbor, followed by Hadar.[273]

The children of Israel listed in Genesis as having moved to Egypt from Canaan numbered seventy including Joseph and his sons and excluding Israel and the wives of his sons. The initial company of Israel coming to Egypt included Kohath the son of Levi, great grandfather and grandfather of Moses, Aaron and Miriam. Moses' mother was Jochebed, daughter of Levi. She was born in Levi's sixty fourth year of sixteen years after Israel settled his family in Egypt, according to the Testament of Levi. This same record reported that Amram, grandson of Levi and father of Moses was born to Kohath on the same day as Jochebed. Jochebed and Amram were married at age thirty in Levi's ninety fourth year.[274]

The lives of each son of Israel and his relationship to the Lord God Jehovah are summarized in the chapters that follow in the believed order of their deaths, rather than the order of their births.

---

271. Genesis 36:32; Jasher LVII:1-45
272. Jasher LVIII:1-30
273. Genesis 36:31-43
274. Testament of Levi III:35-58 The Forgotten Books of Eden

CHAPTER XIX

JOSEPH, SON OF ISRAEL AND RACHEL

Israel was ninety one and Rachel was about thirty five years old when Joseph was born. Israel and his family, including the newly born Joseph, stayed in Padan Aram another six years while the Lord worked wonders with speckled and spotted cattle and sheep which became the property of Israel. Joseph was six years old when Israel, Leah, Rachel, Bilhah, Zilpah and their twelve children left for Canaan.

Rachel died when Joseph was about nine years old. Israel and his family, along with Joseph, were enroute to visit Isaac. As they approached Ephrath or Bethlehem Rachel travailed and died giving birth to Benjamin, Israel's thirteenth child and twelfth son. Rachel was buried near Ephrath. Her grave was marked by a pillar.[275]

Abraham, Isaac and Israel each had conferred upon them three great blessings from God: the rights of priesthood, kings and birth, sometimes referred to as the crowns of priesthood, kings and gospel (Torah) as previously mentioned. In connection with these three great blessings, men were/are permitted to act for God, not to achieve their vain ambitious or to gratify their personal pride, or to control or compel the souls of the children of men in any degree of unrighteousness. Rather, those who hold these powers were/are to let personal righteousness be the guiding principle in handling or controlling them. These powers were/are given to men to assist God in achieving His purposes which include the bringing to pass the immortality and eternal life of mankind, and the blessing of the lives of others.[276]

Failure to let personal righteousness be the guiding principle in his life caused Reuben, Israel's first born son, to forfeit the rights of birth, priesthood and kings. Joseph, firstborn of Israel's second wife, by contrast, would later prove to the Lord's satisfaction that personal righteousness was the guiding principle in his life. The birthright blessings were conferred upon Joseph, the priesthood upon Levi and the right of Kings upon Judah, after Reuben had forfeited them by defiling his father's bed.

There was more to Israel's love for Joseph than the fact that he was a son of his old age. Benjamin, as a matter of fact, was the last of his sons to be born. Joseph's selection as heir to the birthright blessings, following Reuben's forfeiture of them, likely contributed to the perception that Israel favored Joseph over his other sons.

Younger than ten of his brothers, Joseph did not participate in their battles with the Canaanites. Judah, heir to the kingly blessings, led his brothers and their servants in these, and in effect, saved the family of Israel from destruction. Their fame, and particularly that of Judah, spread throughout the land.

Judah, heir to the kingly blessings, had already begun to function in a role perceived to be that of king, i.e. to be the best and valiant of warriors leading others in battle. Levi had had the right of priesthood conferred upon him at age nineteen, according to the Testament of Levi. Joseph's role, as heir to the birthright blessings, by contrast, was deferred. The first evidences of Joseph's special role, and the special role of his posterity, were conveyed by father Israel's treatment of him.

His brother's envy of him, however, was contained until Joseph shared with them two of his dreams, dreams in which God foretold Joseph's future role as heir to the birthright blessings. First, he saved the Lord's covenant people Israel from a famine of food. Second, Joseph's posterity was/is to save Israel, and all the world from another famine; not a famine of bread or thirst for water, but of hearing the words of the Lord, i.e. learning of the Torah or Gospel of the Lord declared sometime in the future.

Joseph had seen the strength of his brethren and their greatness in battle, and he extolled them for it. However, he extolled himself above his brethren. His brothers hated him for this "and they could not speak peaceably unto him". Chapters V, VI, VIII, X, XI, XII unfold the story of how the Lord first humbled, then exalted Joseph, as His prophecies, first revealed in Joseph's dream, were fulfilled.

We resume the story as Joseph approaches his own death. He assembled his family, left his blessing upon them, and prophesied in the name of the Lord God Jehovah what was in store for the Lord's covenant people and for all the world. He reaffirmed Jacob's (Israel's) prophecy that a prophet would be raised up by the Lord to deliver Israel from their afflictions, and that his name was to be Moses. Joseph prophesied concerning the role of his own descendants, including references to the stick of Judah and the stick of Joseph, which were to be joined together as scriptures for the benefit and blessing of mankind. Ezekial made reference to the stick of Judah and the stick of Joseph in the writings of his day.

The Genesis Account reads:

"And Joseph dwelt in Egypt, he and his father's house; and Joseph lived an hundred and ten years. And Joseph saw Ephraim's children of the third generation: the children also of Machir the son of Manasseh were brought up upon Joseph's knees."[277]

(From JST Genesis) "And Joseph said unto his brethren, I die, and go unto my fathers; and I go down to my grave with joy. The God of my father Jacob be with you, to deliver you out of affliction in the days of your bondage; for the Lord hath visited me, and I have obtained a promise of the Lord, that out of the fruit of my loins, the Lord God will raise up a righteous branch out of my loins; and unto thee whom my father Jacob have named Israel, a prophet; (not the Messiah who is called Shilo;) and this prophet shall deliver my people out of Egypt in the days of thy bondage."[278]

Joseph, son of Israel, prophesied the scattering of Israel sometime after their deliverance from bondage. This deliverance would be by a prophet in Israel whose name had been revealed to Jacob (Israel) and again revealed to Joseph as Moses. The Lord also revealed to Joseph that the scattering of Israel would include the scattering of his own descendants, a branch of Israel who would be broken off and carried into a far country. This branch would be remembered in the covenants of the Lord when the Messiah cometh. The Lord God

Jehovah also revealed to Joseph, son of Israel, that he would raise up a seer from the fruit of Joseph's own loins, who would be great like unto another seer or prophet i.e. Moses, neither of whom had yet been born.

Jehovah promised Joseph that this seer who was to be like unto Moses, was to be of the fruit of Joseph's loins, and his name was also to be called Joseph, after the name of his father. In other words, the Lord revealed the name of this other prophet who was to be like unto Moses. His name: Joseph, son of Joseph.

During the course of these revelations to Joseph, son of Israel, the Lord referred to scriptures which He would command to be written. These scriptures were to be written for the future descendants of Judah to whom the right of kings was given, and for the future descendants of Joseph to whom the birthright blessings had been given. These scriptures were to be joined together and would facilitate the gathering of scattered Israel together sometime in the future.

(From Ezekiel) "The word of the Lord came unto me saying, moreover, thou son of man, take thee one stick and write upon it, For Judah, and for the children of Israel his companions: then take another stick, and write upon it, For Joseph, the stick of Ephraim, and for all the house of Israel his companions: And join them one to another into one stick; and they shall become one in thine hand. And when the children of thy people shall speak unto thee, saying, Wilt thou not show us what thou meanest by these?"

"Say unto them, thus saith the Lord God; Behold I will take the stick of Joseph, which is in the hand of Ephraim, and the tribes of Israel his fellows, and will put them with him, even with the stick of Judah, and make them one stick; and they shall be one in mine hand. And the sticks where upon thou writest shall be in thine hand before their eyes."

"And say unto them, Thus said the Lord God; Behold I will take the children of Israel from among the heathen, whither they be gone and will gather them on every side, and bring them into their own land: And I will make them one nation in the lands upon the mountains of Israel; and one king shall be king of them all; and they shall be no more two nations, neither shall they be divided into two kingdoms anymore at all."²⁷⁹

These revelations of the Lord to Ezekiel had been previously revealed to Joseph, son of Israel some one thousand years earlier, before the bondage of Israel, before the deliverance of Israel from that bondage in Egypt, and before the scattering of Israel. The Lord had spoken to Joseph, son of Israel, of these future events during Joseph's lifetime.²⁸⁰ᵃ

From Ezekiel we learn that scriptures were to be made available to the Lord's covenant people, scriptures important to themselves and to all mankind. These scriptures were to be written by holy prophets as the Lord would command. They would be for the benefit and blessing of the Lords covenant people, particularly, and for all mankind generally. They would be separately written by the lineage of Judah and of Joseph. There were to be two kingdoms of the Lords covenant peoples in Ezekial's days.

The Lord caused Ezekial to prophecy the future joining of scattered Israel together as one nation. These scriptures or sticks were to be instrumental in bringing scattered Israel together. Joseph's descendants through Ephraim having been given the birthright blessing were also given the greater responsibility,even the leadership role. They were/are to facilitate the gathering of scattered Israel. One set of the scriptures the Lord spoke to Joseph, son of Israel and to Ezekial, about, was referred to as the stick of Ephraim.

Speaking to his brethren shortly before his death, Joseph declared that a branch of the house of Israel, even of his own descendants would be broken off and carried into a far country. They would be remembered in the covenants of the Lord's, however. The Messiah would be made manifest unto this branch in the future. A choice seer would be raised up in the Latter Days from Joseph's own loins, to whom the Lord would speak directly, as He was speaking to Joseph.

While conversing directly with Joseph, the Lord spoke alternately of two future prophets which would be raised up, one whose name was to be Moses, and of another prophet who was to be like unto Moses, whose name would be called Joseph, son of Joseph, neither of whom had yet been born.

Speaking to his brethren Joseph, son of Israel declared,

> (From JST Genesis) "And it shall come to pass that they (Israel) shall be scattered again; and a branch shall be broken off, and shall be carried into a far country; nevertheless they shall be remembered in the covenants of the Lord, when the Messiah cometh; for he shall be made manifest unto them in the latter days, in the Spirit of power; and shall bring them out of darkness into light; out of hidden darkness, and out of captivity unto freedom. A seer shall the Lord my God raise up, who shall be a choice seer unto the fruit of my loins."[280]

Continuing to speak to his brethren, Joseph, son of Israel, quoted directly what the Lord had said to him about this new seer who would be his direct descendant. The Lord compared this new seer to Moses whom the Lord would also raise up to deliver the house of Israel from bondage.

> (From JST Genesis) "thus saith the Lord God of my fathers unto me, A choice seer will I raise up out of the fruit of thy loins (the loins of Joseph, son of Israel), and he shall be esteemed highly among the fruit of thy loins; and unto him will I give commandment that he shall do a work for the fruit of thy loins, his brethren. And he, (the choice seer) shall bring them to a knowledge of the covenants which I have made with thy fathers (Joseph's son of Israel's fathers) and he (the choice seer) shall do whatsoever work I shall command him. And I will make him (the choice seer) great in mine eyes, for he shall do my work; and he shall be great like unto him whom I have said I would raise up unto you to deliver my people, O house of Israel, out of the land of Egypt; for a seer will I raise up to deliver my people out of the land of Egypt; and he shall be called Moses. And by this name he shall know that he is thy house, for he shall be nursed by the king's daughter and shall be called her son."[281]

Referring again to the choice seer of Joseph's seed, the Lord continued to declare;

> (From JST Genesis) "And again a seer will I raise up out of the fruit of thy loins, and unto him will I give power to bring forth my word unto

the seed of thy loins; and not to bringing forth my word only, saith the Lord, but to the convincing of them of my word, which shall have already gone forth among them in the last days."[282]

Not only would this choice seer bring forth God's word to Joseph's descendants through Ephraim and Manasseh, these descendants would believe or be convinced of its truth in the last days.

Continuing to discuss his future plans with Joseph the Lord revealed his intentions to command the fruit of Judah's loins and the fruit of Joseph's loins to write scripture. These Scriptures would grow together to confound false doctrines, lay down contentions and establish peace among Joseph's descendants, and bring them to a knowledge of the Lord's covenants in the last days. The name of the choice seer coming from Joseph, son of Israel's loins was to be Joseph, son of Joseph or Joseph Jr. as previously mentioned. The Lord added that this seer, Joseph, the son of Joseph would bring God's people unto salvation through the scriptures which he would introduce to the world. The Lord then returned to his description of another seer, the one who would be raised up to deliver Israel from Egyptian bondage. He referred to a rod which Moses would use to smite the waters of the Red Sea, and to the law which the Lord would write with His own finger, and to Aaron who was to be Moses' spokesman.

All these things were revealed to Joseph, son of Israel, who even the Pharaoh recognized as a prophet seer and revelator of God.

The actual report from JST Genesis:

"Wherefore the fruit of thy loins shall write, and the fruit of the loins of Judah shall write; and that which shall be written by the fruit of thy loins, and also that which shall be written by the fruit of the loins of Judah, shall grow together unto the confounding of false doctrines, and laying down of contentions and establishing peace among the fruit of thy loins, and bringing them to a knowledge of their fathers in the latter days; and also to a knowledge of my covenants, said the Lord."

"And out of weakness shall he be made strong, in that day when my work shall go forth among all my people, which shall restore them, who are of the house of Israel, in the latter days. And that seer will I bless, and they that seek to destroy him shall be confounded; for this promise I give unto you; for I will remember you from generation to generation; and his name shall be called Joseph, and it shall be after the name of his father; and he shall be like unto you (Joseph, Son of Israel); for the thing (scriptures) which the Lord shall bring forth by his hand shall bring my people unto salvation."

"And the Lord sware unto Joseph that he would preserve his seed forever, saying, I will raise up Moses, and a rod shall be in his hand, and he shall gather together my people, and he shall lead them as a flock, and he shall have judgement, and shall write the word of the Lord, and he shall not speak many words, for I will write unto him my law by the finger of mine hand. And I will make a spokesman for him, and his name shall be called Aaron."[283]

Bearing witness that these prophecies of things to come in the future were true, Joseph, son of Israel, closed his life at age one hundred and ten. He called upon the children of Israel to promise him they will carry his bones out of Egypt and bury them with his fathers Abraham, Isaac, and Israel in Canaan when the day of exodus comes. To facilitate the keeping of this promise, the children of Israel didn't bury Joseph in the customary way. His interment made his body readily assessable, so that when the time came it could be easily retrieved and taken with them.

(From JST Genesis) "And it shall be done unto thee in the last days, also, even as I have sworn. Therefore, Joseph said unto his brethren, God will surely visit you, and bring you out of this land, and unto the land which he swore unto Abraham, and unto Isaac, and to Jacob. And Joseph confirmed many other things unto his brethren, and took an oath of the children of Israel, saying unto them, God will surely visit you, and ye shall carry up my bones from thence."

"So Joseph died when he was an hundred and ten years old, and they embalmed him, and they put him in a coffin in Egypt; and he was kept from burial by the children of Israel, that he might be carried up and laid in the sepulchre with his father. And thus they remembered the oath which they sware unto him."[284]

The Testament of Joseph adds that the promise to carry Joseph's bones to Canaan also included a promise to carry Asenath's bones and bury them near Rachel's in Ephrath.

Reviewing his life at its end Joseph reportedly declared:

(From the Testament of Joseph) "My brethren, and my children, hearken to Joseph the beloved of Israel, give ear my sons unto your father. I have seen in my life envy and death, yet I went not astray, but perservered in the truth of the Lord. These my brethren hated me, but the Lord loved me: They wished to slay me, but the God of my fathers guarded me;
They let me down into a pit and the Most High brought me up again;
I was sold into slavery, and the Lord of all made me free;
I was taken into captivity and His strong hand succoured me;
I was beset with hunger, and the Lord himself nourished me;
I was alone, and God comforted me;
I was sick, and the Lord visited me;
I was in prison, and my God showed favor unto me;
In bonds, and He released me;
Slandered and He pleaded my cause;
Bitterly spoken against by the Egyptians and he delivered me;
Envied by my fellow slaves, and He exalted me."

"I struggled against a shameless woman, urging me to transgress with her, but the God of Israel my father delivered me from the burning flame...."

"I remembered the words of my father....I wept and prayed unto the Lord, and I fasted...."

"For God loveth him who in a den of wickedness combines fasting with chastity, rather than the man who in king's chambers combines luxury with license.
    Ye see, therefore, my children how great things patience worketh, and prayer with fasting.
    So ye too, if ye follow after chastity and purity with patience and prayer, with fasting in humility of heart, the Lord will dwell among you because He loved chastity.
    And wheresoever the Most High dwelleth, even though envy, or

slavery, or slander befalleth a man, the Lord dwelleth in him, for the sake of his chastity, not only delivereth him from evil, but also exalteth him even as me,

For in every way the man is lifted up, whether in deed or in word or in thought.

My brethren knew how my father loved me, and yet I did not exalt myself in my mind, although I was a child, I had the fear of God in my heart, for I knew that all things would pass away.

And I did not raise myself against them with evil intent, but I honored my brethren; and out of respect for them even when I was being sold, I refrained from telling the Ishmaelites that I was a son of Jacob, a great man and a mighty (one),

Do ye also my children have the fear of the God in all your works before your eyes, and honor your brethren. For every one who doeth the law of the Lord shall be loved by him."[285]

The Testament of Joseph continues the story of Joseph's suffering as a new slave, and Joseph's behavior related thereto.

"Ye see, therefore, my children, what great things I endured that I should not put my brethren to shame. Do ye also, therefore love one another, and with long suffering hide ye one anothers faults.   For God delighteth in the unity of brethren, and in the purpose of a heart that takes pleasure in love, and when my brethren came unto Egypt they learnt that I had returned their money unto them, and upbraided them not, and comforted them. And after the death of Jacob my father, I loved them more abundantly. And all things whatsoever he commanded I did very abundantly for them. And I suffered them not to be afflicted in the smallest matter; and all that was in my hand I gave unto them.

And their children were my children, and my children as their servants; and their life was my life, and all their suffering was my suffering, and all their sickness was my infirmity. My land was their land, and their counsel my counsel. And I exalted not myself among them in arrogance because of my worldly glory, but I was among them as one of the least."

"If ye also, therefore, walk in the commandments of the Lord, my children, He will exalt you there, and will bless you with good things forever and ever. And if any one seeketh to do evil unto you, do well unto him, and pray for him and ye shall be redeemed of the Lord from all evil."[286]

Joseph shared with those assembled a vision of the future in which he saw the Lamb of God who would be born of Judah's and Levi's loins, the Messiah. He would take away the sins of the world and save the Gentiles as well as all Israel from their sins. Joseph closed his testimony and life with a prophecy that his (Joseph's) kingdom would end. The Egyptians would afflict Israel, but God would bring them out of Egypt and back to the land of their fathers in Canaan.

The Testament of Joseph report:

"And hear ye, my children, also the vision which I saw. There were twelve harts feeding: And the nine were first dispersed over all the earth, and likewise also the three.

And I saw that from Judah was born a virgin wearing a linen garment, and from her was born a lamb, without spot; and on his left hand there was as it were a lion; and all the beasts rushed against him, and the lamb overcame them, and destroyed them and trod them under foot. And because of him the angels and men rejoiced, and all the land. And these things shall come to pass in their season, in the last days.

Do ye therefore, my children, observe the commandments of the Lord, and honor Levi and Judah; for from them shall arise unto the Lamb of God, who taketh away the sin of the world, one who saveth all the Gentiles and Israel. For his kindgom is an everlasting kingdom, which shall not pass away; but my kingdom among you shall come to an end as a watcher's hammock, which after the summer disappeareth. For I know that after my death the Egyptians will afflict you, but God will avenge you, and will bring you unto that which he promised to your fathers. But ye shall carry up my bones with you; for when my bones are being taken up thither, the Lord shall be with you in light and Beliar shall be in darkness with the Egyptians. And carry ye up Asenath your mother to the Hippedrome, and near Rachel your mother bury her. And when he had said these things, he stretched out his feet and died at a good old age."[287]

For a more complete description see The Testament of Joseph in The Forgotten Books of Eden P. 259-266, in the Old Testament Pseudepigrapha P. 819-825 and/or Joseph, The Favorite Son, The Legends of the Jews II P. 3-184.

275.	Genesis 35:16-20; Jasher XXXVI:9-12
276.	Doctrine and Covenants 121:39-46
277.	Genesis 50:22-23 KJV, MT, JST
278.	JST Genesis 50:24
279.	Ezekial 37:15-22 KJV, MT, JST
280A.	Genesis JST 50:31
280.	JST Genesis 50:25-26
281.	Ibid 50:27-29
282.	Ibid 50:30
283.	Ibid 50:31-35
284.	Ibid 50:36-38
285.	Testament of Joseph I:1-81, II:1-8
286.	Ibid II:58-68
287.	Ibid II:72-82
	Testament of Joseph, The Forgotten Books of Eden P. 259-266
	Testament of Joseph, The Old Testament Pseudepigrapha P. 819-825
	Legends of the Jews II Joseph the Favorite Son P. 3-184

Chapter XX

ZEBULUN, SON OF ISRAEL

Zebulun was born the sixth son of Israel and Leah in Haran or Padan Aram. He reportedly went to Midian and took a wife named Merushah, daughter of Molad, the son of Abida, the son of Midian, the son of Abraham and brought her to Canaan. Merushah bore unto Zebulun three sons: Sered, Elan, and Yachlel.[288]

Being the sixth son, Zebulun was closest in age to Joseph of all of Leah's sons. From the Testament of Zebulun it appears that he was not fully aware of the sin which was committed against Joseph. He was greatly influenced by his older brothers. They had all covenanted not to tell father Israel what they had done. They had agreed that if any one should declare the secret, he would be slain. Zebulun pled with them not to slay Joseph.

Apparently Simeon and Gad came against Joseph to slay him. In tears Zebulun listened as Joseph pled for his own life, saying,

> "Pity me, my brethren, have mercy upon the bowels of Jacob our father: Lay not upon me your hands to shed innocent blood, for I have not sinned against you. And if indeed I have sinned, with chastening chastise me, my brethren, but lay not upon me your hand, for the sake of Jacob, our father."[289]

Zebulun was unable to bear Joseph's lamentations, and began to weep. His body trembled and he could not stand. Meanwhile, Reuben took the lead in convincing them Joseph should be cast into the pit instead of being slain. They did so. While Reuben was off looking for feed for their animals, his brethren sold Joseph.

Zebulun was so sick from what they had done, he could not eat, though his brethren did. He watched the pit, fearing Simeon, Dan, and Gad would rush off and slay Joseph. Zebulun watched the pit until Joseph was sold to the Ishmaelites. When Reuben returned and heard what his brothers had done, he rent his garments, and ran after the Ishmaelites with the money, intending to buy Joseph back. It was too late. He couldn't find them and so he returned grieving. Reuben also would not eat that day.

Dan came to the grieving Reuben counseling him not to grieve, for they had found what to say to father Israel. "Let us slay a kid of the goats, and dip in it the coat of Joseph; and let us send it to Jacob ....and they did so.[290]

Zebulun refused to accept any of the money they got from the sale of Joseph. Simeon and Gad and some of the other brothers each took the price of Joseph and bought sandals for themselves, their wives and children. They didn't want to purchase food with the money. Instead they symbolically tred him under foot with their sandals, because Joseph had said he would be king over them, "So let us see what will become of his dreams."[291]

Apparently Zebulun earned his living from the sea and had an affinity for ships. Fish formed a significant portion of his diet. Israel's blessing of Zebulun states, "Zebulun shall dwell at the haven of the sea, and he shall be for an haven of ships, and his border shall be unto Zidon."[292]

As Zebulun approached the end of his life he assembled his sons, counselled them to keep the commands of God, to show mercy to their neighbors, and to have compassion towards all, both to humans and to beasts. He related his own experiences in providing compassionate service when his brethren were sick, saying: "even as a man doeth to his neighbour, even so also will the Lord do to him." He broiled fish, dressed them and offered them to men in need or those who were grieving, explaining, "he that shareth with his neighbour receiveth manifold more from the Lord."

Zebulun fished in the summer and kept sheep with his brethren in the winter, giving generously food and clothing to his neighbours and friends who were in need. He counseled his children not to hesitate in showing compassion and mercy to all men saying: "for in the degree in which a man hath compassion upon his neighbours, in the same degree hath the Lord also upon him."[293]

Zebulun reported that Joseph showed no malice towards his brethren when they went down to Egypt. He counseled his children to show no malice towards each other but to love one another. He encouraged unity among them, comparing them to waters when they flow together they sweep along powerfully stones, trees, earth and other things. When divided into many streams the earth swallows up the water and it vanishes.

Having read the writings of his fathers Israel, Isaac and Abraham, Zebulun learned from prophecies contained therein that Israel would be divided into two kingdoms, would follow two kings, would work abominations and be led into captivity.

He reiterated prophecies contained in these writings or scriptures of his fathers, that after falling away the children of Israel would remember the Lord and repent. God would be merciful and compassionate towards the repentant, recognizing weaknesses of the flesh. Zebulun affirmed his conviction that the Messiah would come, whom he referred to as the light of righteousness.

Zebulun asked his children to grieve not for him. He assured them he would rise in the resurrection and be a ruler in the midst of his sons (posterity) rejoicing in the midst of the members of this tribe who keep the law of the Lord.

Calling upon them to fear the Lord our God with all their strength all the days of their lives, he fell asleep at a good old age (114). He was laid in a wooded coffin and afterwards was carried from Egypt and buried in Hebron with his fathers.[294]

For a more complete description see The Testament of Zebulun in The Forgotten Books of Eden p. 244-247, in The Old Testament Pseudipigrapha p. 805-807 and/or Zebulun Exhorts Unto Compassion, The Legends of the Jews p. 204-207.

288. Jasher XLV:19-20, Genesis 46:15
289. Testament of Zebulun I:1-12
290. Ibid I:13-37
291. Ibid I:19
292. Genesis 49:13 KJV, MT, JST
293. Testament of Zebulun I:1-21
294. Ibid II 29-42

Chapter XXI

SIMEON, SON OF ISRAEL

Simeon was born the second son of Israel and Leah. Leah called him Simeon because the Lord had heard her prayer. The family had been moved by Israel from Padan Aram to the outskirts of Canaan, then on to Shechem where he had bought land for his family and animals.

Simeon was a central figure in the events surrounding the tragedy of Dinah. Fired with anger when they heard that Dinah had been kidnaped, raped, and held against her will, Simeon and his brothers sought to get even. Reportedly, it was Simeon who suggested all the males be circumcised as a means to bring them into subjection. When Hamor and Shechem and all the others were sunk down with pain the teenage sons of Israel would attack and kill them. The men of Shechem took the bait and were circumcised:

> (From Genesis) "Simeon and Levi, Dinah's brethren, took each man his sword, and came upon the City boldly, and slew all the males. And they slew Hamor and Shechem his son with the edge of the sword, and took Dinah out of Shechems house and went out."[295]

Israel was not pleased with their works, being afraid their actions would bring all the kings of Canaan against them. Simeon and Levi called their father to task for not speaking out against Shechem's actions. "Shall he deal with our sister as with a harlot in the streets?"[296]

Among those taken captive by Simeon and Levi during this encounter with Shechem was a young maiden of Canaan named Bunah. Simeon reportedly married her shortly after she was taken captive. He later married his sister Dinah, and all his children were born of Bunah and Dinah according to some sources.

Simeon's strength and prowess in battle were soon recognized by the people of Canaan. His battle tactics included letting out loud and tremendous shrieks. These shrieks unnerved the Canaanites and helped the sons of Israel to prevail over them. When angered and his system was full of adrenalin, Simeon could hardly be contained.

During his final days he admitted he was jealous of Joseph and had sought to destroy him. Blinded by this jealousy Simeon took the lead in counsel with his brothers to kill Joseph and be rid of the dreamer. A different view prevailed. Joseph was placed in the pit. Reuben went to get food for the animals. Simeon was dispatched to Shechem to get ointment for the flock. While they were gone Judah sold Joseph.

Upon his return Simeon became exceedingly angry with Judah for selling Joseph. Simeon wanted Joseph dead. His wrath against Judah lasted four months. He was humbled, however. The Lord caused Simeon's right hand to become half withered and almost useless and caused his strength to dry up.

Reporting his experiences to his children Simeon was supposed to have said,

> (From the Testament of Simeon) "And I knew, my children, that because of Joseph this had befallen me, and I repented and wept, and I besought the Lord God that my hand might be restored, and that I might hold aloof from all pollution, and envy and from folly....And now, my children, hearken unto me and beware of the spirit of deceit and envy. For envy ruleth over the whole mind of a man, and suffereth him neither to eat nor to drink nor to do any good thing. But it ever suggesteth to him to destroyeth him that envieth; and so long as he that is envied flourisheth, he that envieth fadeth away."[297]

Simeon went on to report that he fasted periodically over a two year span seeking deliverance from envy. He concluded that deliverance from envy comes when the person really fears (loves) the Lord. When that happens the Lord forgives.

Simeon was the one who was left in Egypt as surety for Benjamin when the rest of his brothers were allowed to return to Canaan during the seven year famine. At this stage of his life Simeon was subdued and accepted his lot as just payment for his earlier desire and attempts to have Joseph slain. His experience in Egypt with Joseph while his brothers were back in Canaan caused Simeon to recognize Joseph as a good man filled with the spirit of God, a compassionate man, bearing no malice toward Simeon or his brothers. Simeon counseled his children to love each one his brothers with a good heart, and the spirit of envy will depart from them.

Having had first hand experience with envy and jealousy, Simeon said these two cause anger and war in the mind and stirs up deeds of blood, leading the mind into frenzy, causing tumult of the soul and trembling of the body. Even in sleep malicious jealousy gnaws on the soul, causes the body to be troubled, and awakens the mind from sleep in confusion. He counseled his children to make their hearts good before the Lord and their ways straight before men.

He counselled them to beware of fornication, calling fornication the mother of all evils, evils which separate those who commit fornication from God and bring them to Satan. Citing the writings of Enoch as the source of this counsel Simeon reiterated prophecies contained therein that some of the Lord's covenant people would be corrupted by fornication.

Peering into the future by way of the scriptures of his day, Simeon forecast the fall of Canaan and the perishing of its people. He declared the coming of a mighty one of Israel who would glorify Shem (Melchizedek?). This mighty one of Israel was to be the Lord God Himself who would appear on earth and Himself save men. The Lord God of Israel Himself would take a body and eat with men. He would be recognized as an High Priest and a King of the loins of both Levi and Judah. He would come to save all Israel and all the Gentiles, as well, from their sins. Simeon counselled his children to obey Levi and Judah declaring from them shall arise the salvation of God.

Simeon commanded his children to teach their children and subsequent generations these things. When he had made an end of commanding his children he slept with his fathers being an hundred and twenty years old. They laid him in a wooden coffin. Later they took his bones to Hebron, secretly during a war of the Egyptians. Apparently the bones of Simeon and several of his brothers were taken to Hebron at one time, before the general exodus of the children of Israel from Egypt.

Joseph's bones were not taken until the general exodus, for they were apparently guarded by the Egyptians. Egyptian sorcerers had let it be known that on the departure of the bones of Joseph there would be darkness and gloom in all Egypt, so much so that even with a lamp a man should not recognize his brother. Exceeding great plagues would also accompany such departure. Hence, Joseph's bones were guarded by the Egyptians to prevent these things from happening.

Simeon's death was mourned by his children. Their descendants were among those of Israel who departed Egypt at the general exodus led by Moses years later.[298]

For a more complete description see The Testament of Simeon in The Forgotten Books of Eden p. 224-226 The Old Testament Psuedepigrapha p. .pa 785-788 and Simeon's Admonition Against Envy in The Legends of the Jews II p. 191-194.

---

295. Genesis 34:25-29 KJV, MT, JST
296. Jasher XXXIV:32-34
297. Testament of Simeon I:12-17
298. Testament of Simeon I, II, III

Chapter XXII

REUBEN, SON OF ISRAEL

Reuben was the first born son of Israel and Leah. He would ordinarily have been heir to the birthright, priesthood and kingly blessings possessed by Israel, his father. Reuben lost these blessings through transgression as previously mentioned. This loss overshadowed other events in Reuben's life. There is much to commend in his life, however, and much of which he did was exemplary indeed.

Reuben moved with his family from Padan Aram to Canaan at about age thirteen. The family included father Israel, his mother Leah, three step mothers ten brothers, one sister, many servants and animals. He was probably in his late teens when Rachel died giving birth to Benjamin.

After Rachel's death Israel moved his tent in with Bilhah, and left for a visit with Isaac. While Israel was gone, Reuben, jealous for his mother Leah, defiled his father's bed by sleeping with Bilhah. It took Reuben many years to recover from this transgression and from the loss of the birthright, priesthood and kingly blessings.

By the time Joseph was seventeen, apparently Reuben had clearly repented of his sins, and acted to protect Joseph from the wrath of some of his brothers who had sought to kill him. It was Reuben who suggested Joseph be placed in the pit, instead of being slain. It was Reuben who intended to retrieve Joseph from the pit and return him to his father Israel. He was not present when Judah, acting for his brothers sold Joseph, Reuben would not eat that day, nor would he use money received from Joseph's sale for personal gain. When Reuben learned of the sale, he took the money, and tried to catch up with the Ishmaelites and buy Joseph back. It was too late.

Reuben was the father of four sons, born, according to Jasher, of his wife Eluiram, the daughter of Avi, the Canaanite, who was of Timnah. Reuben and his family accompanied Israel into Egypt. Their children included Hanoch, Phallin, Hezron and Carmi.

As his life drew to a close after the death of Joseph, Reuben assembled his family together. Some of his brothers were still living and were assembled there including Judah, Gad, and Asher. He asked his brother's to raise him up so that he could speak to his family. He kissed them and requested they give heed to what he was about to say.

Reuben counseled his children not to walk in the sins of youth and fornication as he had done when he defiled his father's bed. He bore witness that God smote him with a sore plague in his loins for seven months, and that father Israel had prayed to the Lord for him. Were it not for those prayers, said Reuben, the Lord would have destroyed him. Reuben said that he repented of these sins over a period of seven years.

Most of what Reuben had to say to his family at the close of his life dealt with the sins he had committed. He wanted his family to avoid these sins. He counseled his sons to pay no heed to the beauty of woman. Instead, each should walk in singleness of heart in the fear of God, and expend labor in good works, until the Lord gave him a wife. He explained that he had difficulty looking in the face of his father most of his life, being ashamed of what he had done. Father Israel comforted him, he said, and prayed unto the Lord for him that the anger of the Lord might pass by Reuben.

Reuben said that fornication had destroyed many a man though he be old or noble or rich or poor. A man who commits fornication brings reproach to himself and allows himself to be controlled by Satan. He cited Joseph as a great example of chastity declaring that Joseph purged his thoughts from all fornication and found favor in the sight of God and men.

Reuben reported that the Egyptian woman did many things to seduce Joseph; she had summoned magicians, and offered love potions, but his soul admitted no evil desire. Reuben assured his sons that Satan could not overcome them if they would not yield to fornication. He warned them not be beguiled by women. He counseled his sons wives and his daughters not to make up their faces and adorn their heads to deceive the minds of men or to use their wiles to seduce men.

Reuben commanded his children to hearken unto Levi; because Levi knew the law of the Lord, and His ordinances, reminding them that through Levi and his posterity sacrifices for all Israel would be made until the consummation of the times, or until the Lord comes. He adjured them by the God of Heaven to be truthful with one another and with their neighbors, and to love one another. He advised them to receive priesthood blessings from Levi and to honor Judah and his posterity to whom the right of kings was given.

Reuben died and they placed him in a coffin and carried him up from Egypt and buried him with his father Israel.[299]

For a more complete description see The Testament of Reuben in The Forgotten Books of Eden, p. 220-223, The Old Testament Pseudepigrapha p. 782-785 and Reubens Testament in the Legends of the Jews p. 189-191.

---

299. Testament of Reuben I, II

CHAPTER XXIII

DAN, SON OF ISRAEL

Dan was born in Padan Aram, the first son by Bilhah, and probably the sixth or seventh in order of birth of all Israel's sons. Dan reportedly went to the land of Moab and took for a wife Aphlaleth, the daughter of Chamudan the Moabite, and brought her to the land of Canaan. From Aphlaleth one son, Hushim, was born unto Dan. Hushim was deaf and dumb, according to some sources.

Toward the end of his life Dan reportedly confessed his part in his brother's conspiracy to destroy Joseph. He was relieved, however, when the decision was made to sell rather than kill Joseph. Much of what is written of Dan related to his struggle to overcome his jealousy of Joseph.

Dan said that the jealousy and vanity he felt allowed Satan to influence him. Satan encouraged him to take a sword and slay Joseph. He reasoned that with Joseph dead, Israel would love him (Dan) more. God, however, did not suffer or allow Joseph to fall into Dan's hands, or allow Joseph to be alone with Dan long enough for the deed to be done.

Dan counselled his children to keep themselves from the spirit of lying and anger and to love truth and long suffering instead. Unless they did so, they would perish. He also counselled his children to observe the commandments of the Lord, to keep His law, to speak truth each one to his neighbor, to love the Lord throughout their lives, and to love one another with a true heart.

Dan reportedly had revealed to him something concerning the future of his family: They would depart from the Lord, provoke Levi's posterity and fight losing battles with Judah's posterity. Dan's posterity would be led away into captivity. They would forget their God, be alienated from the land of their inheritance, from the race of

Israel, and from the family of their seed. Adversity would eventually cause them to return to the Lord's ways in the last days.

They were/are to be saved by the Lord who was born of Judah and of Levi. He would turn disobedient hearts unto Him and give them that call upon Him eternal peace. They were/are to rest in Eden, and in the New Jerusalem where the righteous rejoice. The Lord was/is to come and live amongst men. He was/is to be known as the Holy One of Israel, and also as the very angel of peace, who was/is to serve as a mediator between God and man.

Dan counselled his children to fear the Lord and draw near unto God (the Eternal Father) and unto the angel of peace (his son) that intercedeth for them. He told them that His name (the Holy One of Israel) shall be in every place in Israel, and even among the Gentiles. Dan admonished his children to keep themselves from every evil work, to cast away wrath and lying and love truth and long-suffering instead. He urged them to teach their own children these things, especially that they be ready so that the Savior of the Gentiles will receive them.

"Depart, therefore, from all unrighteousness, and cleave unto the righteousness of God, and your race shall be saved forever."

We see from these remarkable prophecies that the Savior of Israel was/is to be the Savior of all mankind, including the Gentiles, or those not of the House of Israel, that he was/is to serve as a mediator between God and mankind, and that there was/is to be a New Jerusalem near Eden, where, in the last days, the tribe of Dan was/is to be gathered.

Dan fell asleep in a good old age. He was buried first in Egypt and later with his father's Abraham, Isaac and Israel in Hebron.[300]

For a more complete description, see The Testament of Dan in The Forgotten Books of Eden p. 247-250, The Old Testament Pseudipigrapha p. 808-810, and Dan's Confession in the Legends of the Jews II, p. 207-208.

---

300. Testament of Dan I, II

CHAPTER XXIV

ISSACHAR, SON OF ISRAEL

Issachar was the fifth son born unto Israel and Leah in Padan Aram. Reuben, probably less than five years old at the time, had been in the wheat field at harvest. He found mandrakes in the field and brought them to his mother Leah. Leah and Rachel believed the mandrakes, if eaten or otherwise used, would increase a woman's fertility.

Believing the mandrakes would relieve her barrenness, Rachel took them from Reuben. Reuben wept, and the sound of his voice brought Leah. A dispute over the mandrakes followed. Rachel wanted to keep them. Recognizing Reuben had found them, she said to Leah, "give me, I pray thee, of thy sons mandrakes."[301] Leah countered by accusing Rachel of taking her husband Israel, and now would she take her son's mandrakes also?

Leah had had four sons, Reuben, Simeon, Levi, and Judah, and had left bearing temporarily. Apparently, Israel was living in the tent of Rachel, which Leah resented. Rachel struck a deal with Leah. Israel would stay with Leah that night, if Leah would consent to have Rachel retain the mandrakes. Leah must have agreed, for she approached Israel that evening and said, "Thou must come in unto me, for surely I have hired thee with my son's mandrakes. And he lay with her that night."[302]

Leah conceived and Issachar was born from that union.

The Testament of Issachar identified the mandrakes as sweet smelling apples which grew below a ravine of water in Haran. During the discussion over them, Leah had supposedly boasted of her superior status as Israel's first wife. Rachel countered by saying Israel had worked fourteen years for her, Rachel. Further, that it was by craft or trick, that Leah had been Israel's first wife. Israel had preferred Rachel as a wife. Rachel proposed Israel sleep with Leah in exchange for the mandrakes. The name Issachar somehow is connected with the hiring of Leah for that night.

An angel reportedly visited Israel shortly after this incident and informed him that Rachel would bear two sons. Rachel had given up an opportunity to sleep with Israel for the sake of the mandrakes. She had demonstrated for the sake of children she wished to company with Israel, and not for lust or pleasure. Rachel reportedly did not eat the mandrakes. Instead, she offered them to the Lord pleading that somehow she would conceive.

It was Leah who conceived again, immediately. Issachar was soon born. He became a husbandman for his father Israel. He brought forth much in fruits from the field according to their season. Issachar was generous with these fruits of the field, giving to the poor and needy.

Issachar, the husbandman, was referred to as a hard worker by his father Israel in these words:

> "Issachar is a strong ass, couching down between two burdens. And he saw that rest was good, and the land was pleasant and bowed his shoulder to bear, and became a servant unto tribute."[303]

Issachar reportedly accompanied his brother Levi to the land of the east and took for a wife, the daughter of Jobab, the son of Yoktan, the son of Eber, and her name was Aridah. And Aridah bore unto Issachar, Tola, Puvah, Job, and Shamron, four sons.

Issachar apparently did not seek power or glory, or the vain things of life. He counseled his children to shun envy, evil, maliciousness, and to walk in guilelessness, to love the Lord and their neighbors, and to have compassion on the poor and the weak. He counselled them to toil in the labors of the field and to offer the first fruits of the earth to God, and He, the Lord God, would bless them as He had blessed all His followers from Abel until "now."

Issachar reminded them to obey Levi and Judah who had received the priesthood and kingly blessings. He prophesied that his posterity would forsake the way's of the Lord and His commandments and would follow wickedness. As a consequence, his posterity or the tribe of Issachar would be dispersed among the Gentiles and would end up as servants of their enemies. Issachar's posterity, however, would eventually return to the Lord. The Lord would be merciful and would deliver them to their land of inheritance in the last days.

As he closed his life Isaachar declared he had been true to his wife, had not drunk wine, or coveted anything of his neighbors. He had not lied nor had guile arose in his heart. He had shared his bread with the poor and had loved the Lord and every man with all his heart. He counselled his children to do likewise.

He commanded them to carry his body out of Egypt to Hebron in Canaan and bury him with his father's Abraham, Isaac and Israel. He stretched out his feet and died. His children carried out his wishes.[304]

For a more complete description, see the Testament of Issachar in The Forgotten Books of Eden p. 241-243, the Old Testament Pseudepigrapha p. 802-804, and Issachar's Singleness of heart, in the Legends of the Jews II p. 201-204.

---

301. Genesis 30:14 KJV, MT, JST
302. Ibid 30:15-16 KJV, MT, JST
303. Ibid 49:14-15
304. Testament of Issachar I, II

Chapter XXV

ASHER, SON OF ISRAEL

Asher was born the second son of Israel and Zilpah, the handmaid of Leah. His name meant happy or blessed. After Joseph had been sold into Egypt, Asher reportedly took Adon, the daughter of Aphlal, the son of Hadad, the son of Ishmael for a wife. She died, however, without offspring. After Adon died, Asher crossed the river and took a widow for a wife. Her name was Hadurah, the daughter of Abimael, a descendant of the son of Eber and of Shem. She had been the wife of Malkiel, a descendant of Elam and of Shem.

Hadurah had given birth to a daughter by Malkiel whose name was Serach or Sarah. After Malkiel died his widow Hadurah married Asher, who was a widower. Asher brought Hadurah to the land of Canaan along with Serach or Sarah, who was about three years old.

Hadurah was described as a young woman of comely appearance and a woman of sense. Her daughter, Serach or Sarah, was also of comely appearance, and was described as a child to whom the Lord gave wisdom and understanding. She grew up in the house of Israel and walked in his sanctified ways. Sarah figured prominently in informing Israel that Joseph was alive and in Egypt. At the request of her uncles, she played the harp and sang a message softly to Israel, declaring Joseph was alive and not dead. When Israel's sons came with beasts laden with gifts from Joseph, he was better prepared for the great news, though the shock was substantial.

Asher was the father of four sons by Hadurah: Jimnah, Ishuah, Isui, and Beriah who came with them into Egypt.

As Israel closed his life some seventeen years later, he blessed his sons including Asher. Israel assured Asher that he and his posterity would always have plenty to eat in these words from Genesis: "Out of

Asher his bread shall be fat, and he shall yield royal dainties."[305]

Asher's counsel to his children and posterity included contrasting good with evil. They were encouraged to keep the commandments of God. He explained that when a soul departs this life troubled, it is tormented by the evil spirit which it served in lust and evil work. On the other hand, the soul that departs in peace, meets the angel of peace (the Savior) who leads him/her into eternal life.

Asher prophesied that his posterity would fall into sin and into the hands of their enemies; that they would be scattered unto the four corners of the earth along with the posterity of Gad and Dan; that they would vanish as water in the desert and would lose their identity as to lands, tribe, and tongue.

He prophesied that the Most High (God) would come Himself as man, eating and drinking, and would have power greater than Satan. He was/is to save all Israel and the Gentiles as well.

After He came/comes to earth, the Lord will gather the posterity of Asher, Gad, Dan and others in faith through His tender mercy for the sake of Abraham, Isaac and Israel.

At the close of his life, Asher asked to be buried in Hebron. He lived to be about 125 years of age, and was eventually buried with his father's as requested.[306]

For a more complete description, see The Testament of Asher in the Forgotten Books of Eden p. 257-259, the Old Testament Pseudepigrapha I p. 816-818, and Asher's Last Words, Legends of the Jews II p. 218-220.

---

305. Genesis 49:20 KJV, MT, JST
306. Testament of Asher I p. 257-259

Chapter XXVI

GAD, SON OF ISRAEL

Gad was born the first son of Israel by Zilpah, the handmaid of Leah. After Joseph had been sold into Egypt, Gad reportedly went to Haran and took a wife, who was the daughter of Amuram, the son of Uz, the son of Nahor. Her name was Uzith, and Uzith reportedly bore unto Gad; Zephion, Uagi, Shumi, Ezgan, Eri, Arodi, and Areli, seven sons.

Apparently Gad was among those who wished to kill Joseph. Gad hated Joseph because of his two dreams. He also felt Joseph had misrepresented some earlier actions. Genesis mentions that Joseph, at age seventeen, had been with the sons of Bilhah (Dan and Naphtali) and the sons of Zilpah (Gad and Asher). Joseph had brought an evil report unto father Israel. No explanation of the "evil" report is given in Genesis. The Testament of Gad elaborates.

Gad and his brothers were shepherds watching over their father's sheep, at night near Shecham, protecting them from wolves and other wild beasts. Joseph reportedly with them for about thirty days, fell sick by reason of the heat, and subsequently returned to his father Israel in Hebron. Joseph, according to Gad, told Israel that the sons of Bilhah and Zilpah i.e. Dan, Naphtali, Gad and Asher were slaying the best of the flocks and eating them, against the advice of Reuben and Judah.

Gad felt Joseph's report was not fair. Defending his actions, Gad acknowledged that he had slain a lamb, but the lamb he slew had been previously captured by a bear. After successfully putting the bear to death, Gad discovered it was so disabled the lamb could not live. The lamb was therefore, killed and eaten by the sons of Bilhah and Zilpah.

The report Joseph gave to Israel so incensed Gad that he wished not to hear of Joseph with his ears or see him with his eyes. Joseph had rebuked them, said Gad, for eating of the flock without Judah's approval. Gad was further angered when it became clear Israel listened to Joseph rather than to them. Gad found it difficult to forgive Joseph for his report. This failure to forgive, cankered Gad's soul during much of his life.

Gad was to overcome the hatred he harbored and overcome his sins, however, after he and his were overpowered by others, for Israel declared, "Gad, a troop shall overcome him; but he shall overcome at the last."[307]

In counseling his children, Gad requested that they hearken to the words of truth, to work righteousness, to live all the law of the Most High, and not to go astray through the spirit of hatred. Hatred, said he, is evil in all the doings of men.

Gad said that those filled with hate despise the truth, envy those who prosper, welcomes evil speaking, and loves arrogance. Hatred, said Gad, blinds the soul. When filled with hatred, a man will not hear the words of God's commandments concerning the loving of one's neighbors; he delights in reporting to others those who stumble, and is quick to demand judgement and punishment of those who have stumbled.

He contrasted love with hatred, saying that as love would quicken even the dead, and would call back them that are condemned to die, so hatred would slay the living, and those who have sinned venially, it would not suffer to live. The spirit of hatred works with Satan and death, while the spirit of love, working with the law of God in long suffering, brings about the salvation of men.

Gad said he was speaking to his children based on his own experience with hatred, which was of the devil, and urged them to cleave to the love of God.

He said that righteousness casts out hatred and humility destroys envy. He that is just and humble is ashamed to do what is unjust, being reproved not of another, but of his own heart. He speaks not against a holy man, because the fear (love) of God overcomes hatred. He would not wrong any man, not even in thought.

Gad said it took him a lifetime to learn those lessons and that he had repented of his thoughts and actions concerning Joseph.

Repentance, said Gad, destroys ignorance, drives away darkness, enlightens the eyes, gives knowledge to the soul and leads the mind to salvation. He counseled his children to love one another in deed and in word, and to put away hatred from their hearts. He urged them to be forgiving of those who transgress against them. They should honor Judah and Levi, said Gad, for from them shall the Lord raise up salvation to Israel.

Gad, too, prophesied that his posterity would fall away and walk in wickedness. Through the blessings of priesthood, kings and birth, however, they would return again to the Lord as scattered Israel is gathered in the last days.

He drew up his feet and fell asleep in peace. His son's buried him in Hebron with his father's five years later.[308]

For a more complete description, see The Testament of Gad, in the Forgotten Books of Eden p.254-256, The Old Testament Pseudipigrapha p. 814-816, and Gad's Hatred in the Legends of the Jews II p. 216-218.

---

307. Genesis 49:19 KJV, MT, JST
308. Testament of Gad, I, II p. 254-256

Chapter XXVII

NAPHTALI, SON OF ISRAEL

Naphtali was born the second son of Israel and Bilhah, the handmaid of Rachel. He had moved with is family from Haran to Canaan. After Joseph had been sold into Egypt, Naphtali went back with Gad, son of Zilpah and Israel, to Haran and took from the daughters of Amuram, the son of Uz, the son of Nahor, Merimah, for a wife. Naphtali brought her back to Canaan. She bore him Yachzeel, Guni, Jazer, and Shalem, four sons.

Bilhah, Naphtali's mother, according to the Testament of Naphtali, was the daughter of Rotheus, the brother of Deborah, Rebecca's nurse. Naphtali was therefore, a descendant of Shem and Eber through his father and through his mother. His mother Bilhah was the daughter of Rotheus, the son of Uz, son of Nahor, son of Terah. Rotheus was described as being of a family of Abraham, a Chaldean, God-fearing and noble. Bilhah's mother reportedly was Euna, a handmaid of Laban. Zilpah was an older sister of Bilhah, and likewise a descendant of Shem and Eber.

All twelve sons of Israel were therefore descendants of Shem and Eber through both their father and their respective mothers: through Israel, son of Isaac, son of Abraham, son of Terah, son of Nahor, son of Serug, son of Reu, son of Peleg, son of Eber, son of Salah, son of Arphaxad, son of Shem, son of Noah; and their mother's Leah and Rachel, daughters of Laban, son of Bethuel, son of Milca and Nahor, son of Terah....; and their mothers Bilhah and Zilpah, daughters of Rotheus, the son of Uz, son of Nahor and Milca, son of Terah....

Merimah, Naphtali's wife was also the daughter of Amuram, the son of Uz, the son of Nahor, the son of Terah, meaning that Naphtali married his cousin.

Naphtali was swift on his feet like a deer. He served his father Israel as a runner, carrying messages on several important journeys: as they battled the Canaanites, for example, and later as a runner for his brother Joseph. He was sent back to Egypt to bring the records of purchase which would prove that Israel owned the cave of Machpelah, having acquired it from his father Isaac, and from his brother Esau.

Israel's blessing compares Naphtali to a hind, or a deer let loose, meaning he indeed was to be swift of foot like a deer. He also would give goodly words. i.e. "Naphtali is a hind let loose; he giveth goodly words."[309]

Napthali reportedly said that the Lord made the physical body of man, after the likeness of the body of man's spirit, one perfectly fitting the other, and that God created every man after His own image. He also declared that God knows men and women and how far each will persist in goodness or evil. No two men or two women were made exactly alike. Each was made a unique creation of the Lord.

Referring to the writings of Enoch, Naphtali reiterated a prophesy that his own posterity would walk in the lawlessness of the Gentiles and do according to all the wickedness of Sodom. His posterity would therefore be taken into captivity. They would serve their enemies and be bowed down with every affliction and tribulation. The members of his posterity would be diminished and be made few, yet those who remained would return to their land according to the abundant mercy of God. After returning to their land of inheritance, the posterity of Naphtali would again forget the Lord and become ungodly.

Naphtali dreamed of a second scattering of all Israel unto the ends of the earth, and of holy writing. He said the Assyrans, Medes, Persians, Chaldeans and Syrians would take in captivity all the twelve tribes of Israel.

Napthali shared his dreams with father Israel. Israel reportedly said to Naphtali he thought Joseph must be alive, because he was included among the twelve tribes whose posterity would be scattered and subsequently gathered. Naphtali said he wanted to tell father Israel that Joseph was not killed by a wild beast, but was sold into Egypt. Naphtali said nothing, however, because he feared his brethren.

Naphtali counseled his children to unite with Levi and Judah, declaring through them shall salvation arise upon Israel, for among their tribes (Levi and Judah) shall God appear dwelling among men on earth to save all Israel.

He encouraged them to work that which is good, to be wise and prudent in understanding the order of God's commandments and His laws. Naphtali had a meal with them, and when he had eaten and drunken with them with a merry heart, he covered his face and died. His sons carried his bones to Hebron and buried them with his fathers.[310]

For a more complete description, see the Testament of Naphtali in The Forgotten Books of Eden p. 250-254, The Old Testament Pseudepigrapha p. 810-814, and Naphtali's Dreams of the Division of the Tribes in the Legends of the Jews II 209-216.

---

309. Genesis 49:21 KJV, MT, JST
310. Testament of Naphtali I, II

Chapter XXVIII

BENJAMIN, SON OF ISRAEL

Benjamin was the second son of Rachel and the last of Israel's children to be born. His eleven brothers and one sister were born in Padan Aram. Benjamin was born after the family had moved to Canaan, near Ephrath or Bethlehem. Benjamin didn't really know his mother. She died giving birth to him. He really didn't know Deborah either, though she had been with Israel's family more than fifteen years. She also had died at about the time Benjamin was born.

Israel's family had moved from Bethel, enroute to visit father Isaac. As they neared Ephrath or Bethlehem, Rachel travailed having hard labor. As her soul was departing Rachel named her new son being born, Benani, or Benjamin, meaning, son of sorrow or distress, or son of the right hand. It is not known who in the family raised Benjamin. Deborah, Rebecca's nurse, was dead, as was Benjamin's mother Rachel. Leah reportedly died when Benjamin was about six. The raising of Benjamin along with his older brother Joseph probably fell to Bilhah, who reportedly suckled Benjamin. Israel had pitched his tent with Bilhah after Rachel's death.

Although the youngest of Israel's sons, Benjamin had fathered the most sons of record by the time the family moved into Egypt. Since Joseph was thirty nine, at the time, Benjamin would have been about thirty years old, as the family moved into Egypt. He brought with him ten sons. He would have had an average of one son per year from age twenty until his move to Egypt. With more than one wife, Benjamin could have fathered his ten sons in a different pattern; such was apparently the case.

Israel had sent to Aram, the son of Zoba, the son of Terah, and he took for his son Benjamin, Mechalia, the daughter of Aram and she came to the land of Canaan to the house of Israel. Benjamin was just ten years old when he was betrothed to Mechalia. Eventually Mechalia bore Benjamin five sons; Bela, Beecher, Ashbed, Gera, and Maaman. At age eighteen, Benjamin took a second wife. She was Aribath, the daughter of Shamron, the son of Abraham. Aribath bore Benjamin five sons also: Achi, Vosh, Mupim, Chupim, and Ord.

Clearly, Benjamin became Israel's favorite son after Joseph had been sold into Egypt. Benjamin stayed behind while Israel's ten other sons were sent to look for Joseph's body which Israel thought had been devoured or mangled by beasts. Benjamin was not part of the conspiracy to conceal the truth of Joseph's whereabouts from Israel.

While his ten brothers were sent to Egypt years later to buy corn, Benjamin, again stayed behind, lest some mischief befall him as it had Joseph. Benjamin was the central figure in the interplay between Joseph, the Pharaoh's second, and his brothers. Joseph had sought to test them. For further details see Chapters XII and XIII.

Benjamin reportedly counseled his children to love the Lord God of heaven and earth, and to keep His commandments. The family of Benjamin was counselled to follow the example of the good and holy man Joseph. They should fear the Lord and love their neighbors, for those who do cannot be smitten by the spirit of Satan, having been shielded by the fear of God. Benjamin said Joseph encouraged father Israel to pray for his brethren, that the Lord would not impute to them as sin, the things they had done to Joseph. He exhorted his children to be followers of Joseph's compassion, and show mercy to all men, even though they be sinners.

Recalling the words of father Israel, Benjamin declared that even though he was scorned and rejected and sold into Egypt by his brethren, Joseph had compassion upon them, and later forgave them, and saved them from the famine of bread. Drawing a parallel to this experience, Benjamin declared that a blameless one, a Lamb of God, would be sent to save all Israel and all the world from the sins of its people. As Joseph was initially rejected by his brethren, scorned and sold, so would this blameless one be initially rejected and delivered into the hands of lawless men. This blameless one would die for ungodly men in the blood of the covenant for the salvation of the Gentiles as well as all Israel.

As Joseph later forgave his brethren so this blameless one, even the Savior, the Son of God, would forgive those who initially rejected and scorned him.

Benjamin encouraged his children and children's children to be followers of this kind of compassion, and not envy those who are glorified by God. Rather, those valiant in following the Lord should be praised, and the virtuous should be lauded. His children were counselled to have mercy on the poor, to have compassion for the weak, and to sing praises unto God. He said that darkness flees away from him who reverences good works.

Benjamin reportedly said that he with a pure mind in love, looks not after a woman with a view of fornication, for he has no defilement in his heart, because the Spirit of God rests in him. For, said he, as the sun is not defiled by shining on dung or mire, but rather dries up both and drives away the evil smell, so also the pure mind though encompassed by the defilements of earth, rather cleans them and is not itself defiled.

He predicted many of his posterity would fall into sin and error, committing fornication and sodomy, and the kingdom of the Lord should be taken away. Nevertheless, the Temple of the Lord would be returned to the posterity of Benjamin later, and that their last Temple shall be more glorious than the first.

Benjamin implied the twelve tribes of Israel would gather together in this new place or country along with the Gentiles and would remain there until the Most High (God) shall send forth His Salvation in the visitation of an holy begotten prophet.

The only begotten prophet of the Father was to enter into the first Temple (at Jerusalem) and there would be treated with outrage and would be lifted upon a tree. The veil of the Temple would be rent following these events, and the Spirit of God would pass on from Israel to the Gentiles. Following the death of this only begotten prophet of God, He would ascend from Hell and pass from the earth into Heaven. He was to be lowly in earth and glorious in Heaven. He would later return and visit the posterity of the twelve tribes of Israel and all the Gentiles in new temples in a new country.

As Benjamin closed his life he counselled his children to keep the commandments of God and endure to the end, until the Lord shall reveal his salvation to all Gentiles. He promised the righteous who keep God's commandments they would eventually see Enoch, Noah, Shem, Abraham, Isaac and Jacob (Israel), rising on the right hand of gladness (God). He promised his righteous posterity they too would rise (be resurrected) worshipping the King of Heaven, who had appeared previously on earth in the form of a man in humility. And as many as believe on Him on the earth, shall rejoice with Him. Then all men shall rise (be resurrected), some unto glory and some unto shame.

The Lord God will judge Israel first, said Benjamin, for their unrighteousness; for when He appeared as God in the flesh to deliver them, they believed Him not. And then He shall judge the Gentiles.

Benjamin implored his children to walk in holiness according to the commandments of the Lord, promising them they would again dwell securely, and all Israel shall be gathered unto the Lord. In that day he, Benjamin, would no longer be called a ravening wolf on account of his posterity's ravages, but rather a worker of the Lord. Apparently this was in reference to Israel's blessing upon Benjamin in which he declared: "Benjamin shall raven as a wolf in the morning he shall devour the prey; and at night shall divide the spoil."[311]

Benjamin reported there shall arise in the latter days one beloved of the Lord, of the tribe of Judah and Levi, a doer of His good pleasure in his mouth with new knowledge enlightening the Gentiles. Until the consumption of the age shall he be in the synagogues of the Gentiles, and among their rulers as a strain of music in the mouth of all. And he shall be inscribed in the Holy books, both his works and his word, and he shall be a chosen one of God, forever.

And through these he shall go to and fro as Jacob my father saying: he shall fill up that which lacketh in thy tribe.

Benjamin closed his life and his sons did as he enjoined them. They took his body and buried it in Hebron with his fathers Abraham, Isaac and Israel.[312]

For a more complete description, see The Testament of Benjamin in The Forgotten Books of Eden p. 266-269, The Old Testament Pseudepigrapha I p. 825-828,and Benjamin Extols Joseph in the Legends of the Jews II p. 220-222.

311. Genesis 49:27 KJV, MT, JST
312. Testament of Benjamin I, II p. 266-269

Chapter XXIX

JUDAH, SON OF ISRAEL

Judah was born in Padan Aram the fourth son of Israel and Leah. As a youth Judah was obedient to his father in everything. He was swift of foot, able to race a hind (deer), catch, kill it and prepare the meat for eating. He was able to overtake a mare, catch it and tame it. Judah's physical strength matched his speed of foot. He slew lions, hurled bears and leopards down cliffs into rocks as they preyed upon his lambs and other animals.

As the sons of Israel battled the Canaanite kings Judah's prowess in combat came more to the fore. He picked up stones of sixty pounds weight and hurled them against Canaanite horses killing same. Nine men in battle array accosted Judah. Slinging stones at them he killed four at once. The rest fled. So powerful was Judah, fear fell upon the Canaanites and they gave up warring against Israel for a while. His partners in battle from time to time included Simeon, Levi, Gad and Dan. Israel saw in visions an angel who followed Judah every where, protecting him when necessary.

As Judah reached manhood father Israel conferred upon him the kingly blessings and assured him he would prosper in all things.

When about twenty years old Judah came in contact with a certain Canaanite identified by the Testament of Judah as Parsaba, king of Adullam, who had a daughter named Bathshua, while visiting his Adullamite friend and employee named Hirah. Hirah (Iram) was apparently working as Judah's chief herdsman. A feast was made by Parsaba, king of Adullam, which Judah attended. Here he met Bathshua, daughter of Parsaba. She became Judah's wife and eventually bore him Er, Onan and Shelah.

In retrospect Judah recognized he should not have married a

Canaanite. Father Israel had not sanctioned his marriage to a Canaanite. This recognition came after Judah's experiences with Bathsua and the death's of Er and Onan.

Er had taken Tamar to wife. Rather than have children by her he spilled his seed upon the ground. The Lord slew him for his wickedness. Onan, his brother, took Tamar to wife after Er's death. Likewise, Onan spilled his seed on the ground rather than have children by Tamar. He also died because his wickedness displeased the Lord. Judah blamed his wife, Bathsua, for the deaths of their sons, Er and Onan. Bathsua apparently didn't want her sons to have children by Tamar, because Tamar was a descendant of Shem rather than of Canaan. Bathsua wanted her grandchildren to worship the idols of Canaan rather than the god of Israel.

Judah tried to marry Shelah, his third son by Bathsua, to Tamar without success. Instead Bathsua secretly arranged Shelah's marriage to a Canaanite. For doing so, Judah reportedly cursed her, and Bathsua died for her wickedness.

About two years following Bathsua's death, Judah made plans to go to Timnath to shear sheep with his friend and chief herdsman Hirah (Iram), the Adullamite. Tamar was told of her father-in-law's plans. She put off her widow's garments, covered herself with a veil, wrapped herself and sat in an open place, which was by the way to Timnath. When Judah saw her, he thought her to be an harlot, because she covered her face.

She apparently realized she would not be married to Shelah, so she took steps to marry according to Amorite law. Compling with one of the idolatrous laws of the Amorites, she adorned herself in Amorite bridal array and sat by the gate of the city of Enaim, near which Judah would pass enroute to Timnath. Those about to marry, according to the idolatrous Amorites, were required to sit in fornication seven days by this gate.

Drunk with wine, thinking Tamar to be a beautiful harlot, the widower of two years, Judah propositioned her by saying, "Let me come in unto thee. "Tamar replied," What wilt thou give me, that thou mayest come in unto me?" Judah responded, "a kid from the flock." Wanting some surety Tamar sought Judah's signet, bracelets and staff (girdle - diadem and staff). They were given to her as surety until the kid of the flock was delivered. Judah went in unto Tamar and she conceived by him. She subsequently put away her vail, and put on the garments of her widowhood again.

Following through with his promise, a kid from the flock was sent to Tamar by way of Judah's Adullamite friend Hirah, with intent to retrieve his surety of signet, bracelets and staff. Tamar was not to be found. About three months later it was told Judah that Tamar, his daughter in law, had played the harlot and was with child by whoredom. Quick to judge, and without realizing he had been a party to the whoredom, he condemned, Judah declared; "Bring her forth and let her be burnt." Tamar confronted Judah by sending the signet, bracelets and staff, saying, she conceived by the man to whom these belonged.

Embarrassed and ashamed, Judah acknowledged them to be his, and also acknowledged what he had done declaring, "She (Tamar) is more righteous than I." He knew Tamar no more. Tamar gave birth to twin sons. They were named Pharez and Zarah. These two sons of Judah and Tamar along with Shelah, son of Judah and Bathsua, gathered to Egypt with Israel during the seven year famine.

Judah figured prominently in the battles Israel fought with the Canaanites, as previously mentioned, and prominently in the events surrounding the movement of Israel into Egypt at Joseph's invitation. He was reportedly forty six years old at the time of the move into Egypt, where he lived another seventy three to eighty three years, depending on which account is used.

Judah advised his children not to follow his example of fornication, which he committed with Bathsua the Canaanite, before his marriage to her; and with Tamar who was espoused and/or married to his sons. He advised them not to get drunk with wine, blaming wine as the major cause of his egregious errors in committing fornication. He said that the spirit of fornication has wine as a minister to give pleasure to the mind, and heats up the body to carnal union.

He blamed wine for causing him to reveal to Bathshua mysteries and commandments of God, and of father Israel, which he, Judah, had covenanted with God not to reveal.

He said that it was the love of money and of beautiful women that caused him to be led astray with Bathshua. Love of money or gold also dethrones the reason of man. Her father had shown Judah much riches which would be given him if he married her. Judah acknowledged his error in marrying a Canaanite without father Israel's approval.

Judah prophesied that because of these two things, money and fornication, his posterity would fall into wickedness. He said that the love of money leads to idolatry, and when led astray through money men name as gods those who are not gods. He declared that the spirit of truth testifieth all things.

Grandfather Isaac and father Israel had blessed Judah to be King of Israel. The Lord gave Judah the kingdom, and to Levi gave he the priesthood, setting the kingdom beneath the priesthood. The kingdom was compared to the things of the earth and the priesthood to things in the heavens. As heaven is higher than the earth, so is the priesthood of God higher than the earthly kingdom, unless the priesthood falls away through sin, and is dominated by the earthly kingdom. Judah counselled his children to love Levi.

Judah foresaw the trials and tribulations of his posterity and counseled his children to repent and walk in all the commandments of God. He promised them if they would do so, they would be brought out of captivity from the Gentiles. He prophesied that a star would arise to his posterity from Jacob (Israel) and from himself, walking in meekness and in righteousness. No sin would be found in Him. The heavens would be opened to Him. The spirit and blessing of God the Eternal Father (Elohim) would be poured out upon Him.

Judah said that the sceptre of his kingdom would shine forth and from their (Judah's) roots shall arise a stem; and from it shall grow a rod of righteousness to the Gentiles, to judge and to save all that call upon the Lord. He prophesied that after these things Abraham, Isaac, and Jacob (Israel) shall arise to life, (be resurrected) and that the twelve sons of Israel shall be chief of the tribes of Israel. In hierarchal terms, Levi and the blessings of the priesthood were to be first, Judah and the earthly kingdom was to be second, Joseph with the birthright blessings was to be third. Identifying particular blessings Judah said the Lord himself blessed Levi; the angel of the Presence blessed Judah; the powers of glory blessed Simeon; the heaven blessed Reuben; the earth blessed Issachar; the sea blessed Zebulun; the mountains blessed Joseph; the tabernacle (tent) blessed Benjamin; the luminaries (lights) blessed Dan; Eden (sleeping) blessed Naphtali; the sun blessed Gad; and the moon (olive tree) blessed Asher.

He said the posterity of Judah would be known as the people of the Lord, and they would have one tongue. Judah counselled his children to observe all the law of the Lord, and declared there is hope for all of them who hold fast unto his ways.

He didn't want them to bury him in costly apparel or to open his bowels (embalm him) as they do with kings. Judah wanted to be buried in Hebron with his father's Abraham, Isaac, and Israel. This did his children as the future unfolded.[313]

For a more complete description, see The Testament of Judah in The Forgotten Books of Eden, p. 233-241, The Old Testament Pseudepigrapha I p. 795-802, and Judah Warns Against Greed and Unchastity in The Legends of the Jews II, p. 198-201

---

313. Testament of Judah p. 233-241

Chapter XXX

LEVI, SON OF ISRAEL

Levi was born the third son of Leah and Israel in Padan Aram. He was first mentioned in Genesis as a participant with Simeon when vengence was wrought upon Hamor for their sister Dinah.

Levi apparently had a dream or vision one day as he was praying that he might be saved from unrighteousness and the corruption of man. It is said that the spirit of understanding of the Lord came to him while he was feeding the flocks at Abel-Maul. Levi reportedly saw three heavens, or three degrees of glory in vision, introduced to him by an angel of God. The second heaven was brighter or more glorious that the first, and the third was more glorious than the second.

The angel that introduced these things said that Levi would be the Lord's minister and would declare God's mysteries to men and would proclaim His role in redeeming all Israel. Levi was also told that this saviour or Messiah would be his descendant and that of Judah. He, the Redeemer, would save every race of men.

The first heaven Levi saw was the lowest of the three and contained the souls of those who had been unrighteous, and who were filled with the spirit of retribution and vengence on men. The second of these heavens contained those souls who would work vengence in behalf of God on those who deserve it in the day of judgement. The Lord God dwelled in the third or highest heaven with all the holy ones.

The angel who visited with Levi told him his prayers had been heard by the Lord, and that he had been forgiven of his sins and for his iniquity. Levi was to become the Lord's servant, and a minister of His presence as well. Levi's posterity would be given a blessing until the Lord visited all the Gentiles in His tender mercies. Levi was to instruct his sons concerning this blessing of priesthood. In other words, an angel revealed to Levi the priesthood or power to act for God would be conferred upon him, and upon his sons, and that they were to be instructed in its use.

As part of the instruction given to Levi, he saw in vision seven men in white raiment saying: "Arise, put on the robe of the priesthood, and the crown of righteousness, and the breastplate of understanding, and the garment of truth, and the plate of faith, and the turban on the head, and the ephod of prophecy." Levi said of the seven men, the first anointed him with holy oil and gave him the staff of judgement, the second washed him with pure water, and fed him with bread and wine, even the most holy things, and clad him with a holy and glorious robe. The third clothed him with a linen vestment like an ephod. The fourth put around him a girdle like unto purple. The fifth gave him a branch of rich olive. The sixth placed a crown upon his head, and the seventh placed on his head a diadem of priesthood, and filled his hands with incense, that he might be a priest before God.

Continuing, the angel informed Levi that his seed would be divided into three offices, for a sign of the glory of the Lord who was to come. The first portion should be great, the second should be in the priesthood, and the third should be called by a new name, because a king should arise in Judah and should establish a new priesthood, and some of these holding the priesthood would be high priests, some judges, and some scribes. Levi said that after this vision or dream had withdrawn from him, he treasured what he had seen in his heart and told no man.

Two days later he and his brother Judah went with father Israel to Isaac their fathers father and that Isaac blessed him (Levi) according to the visions Levi had just seen. Isaac stayed in Beersheba, but Israel and his two sons Levi and Judah returned to Bethel. When they approached Bethel, Israel saw in vision that Levi should become a priest before God, as he, Israel was. Israel rose up early in the morning and paid tithes through his son Levi, the Lord's newly appointed priest.

Later Isaac set about to see that Levi was taught the law of the priesthood, of sacrifices, whole burnt offerings, first fruits, free will, and peace offerings. Isaac counselled his grandson Levi to beware of the spirit of fornication and counselled him to take a wife without blemish, or pollution and one not of the race of strange nations. Before entering the holy place in the tabernacle, Levi was to bathe. He was to wash before offering sacrifice and to wash again after finishing the sacrifice.

Levi and many of his brethren referred to the Book of Enoch the righteous. They quoted from it on occasion. Apparently it contained prophecies concerning the future scattering and eventual gathering of Israel. Levi, referring to the Book of Enoch, declared that his descendants would be taken captive by the Gentiles and they would be under reproach and a curse for a time. He predicted that his posterity would fall into ungodliness and transgression, dealing lawlessly in Israel, after the temple in Jerusalem had been put into operation.

Mindful of the counsel he had received from angels and from grandfather Isaac, and father Israel, Levi took a wife when he was about 28 years of age. Jasher identified her as a descendant of Shem through Eber, the daughter of Jobab, the son of Yoktan, the son of Eber. Her name according to Yashar was Adinah, but the Testament of Levi called her Melcha. Three sons were born to Levi through her, Gersham, Kohath and Merari, and a daughter Jochebed.

Kohath was born when Levi was about thirty five years old. Levi saw special things in vision pertaining to Kohath who eventually became the grandfather of Moses. Kohath was to mark the beginning of majesty and instruction. Levi's wife had difficulty in giving birth to her third son and therefore called him Merari. Levi and his three sons Gersham, Kohath, and Merari, and presumably his wife Adinah came to Egypt with Israel. Jochebed, Levi's daughter, on the other hand, was not born until some sixteen years after Israel arrived in Egypt. She was about a year old when Israel died. Levi was about sixty four years old when Jochebed was born. She reportedly was born the same day as Amram, Levi's grandson and Moses' father by way of Kohath.

Levi reportedly was eight years old when Israel came into Canaan from Padan Aram, eighteen when he slew Shechem, nineteen when he became a priest, twenty eight when he took Adinah to wife, forty eight when he went into Egypt, sixty four when Jochebed was born and one hundred eighteen when Joseph died.

Mindful of what he had seen and heard, Levi counselled his children to work righteousness upon the earth that they might have treasure in heaven, and to sow good things in their souls that they might find them in their lives. He pled with them to avoid those things which would lead them away from the Lord, declaring that whosoever teaches noble things and does them, shall be enthroned with kings, as was Joseph. He counselled that "heaven is purer in the Lord's sight than the earth, so also be ye the light of Israel, purer than the Gentiles."

Levi declared, they would bring a curse upon their tribe by polluting themselves.

Malachi later verified the truth of these prophesies of Levi, for he declared in behalf of the Lord:

> "Know then that I have sent this commandment unto you, that My covenant might be with Levi, Saith the Lord of Hosts. My covenant was with him of life and peace, and I gave them to him, and of fear, and he feared Me, and was afraid of my name. The law of truth was in his mouth, and unrighteousness was not found in his lips; he walked with me in peace and uprightness, and did turn away from iniquity."

> "For the priest's lips should keep knowledge, and they should seek the law of his mouth; For he is the messenger of the Lord of hosts. But ye are turned aside out of the way; ye have caused many to stumble in the law, ye have corrupted the covenant of Levi, saith the Lord of hosts. Therefore have I also made you contemptible and base before all the people, according as ye have not kept my ways; but have had respect of persons in the law."

Continuing Malachi

"....Ye have wearied the Lord with your words. Yet ye say: wherein have we wearied Him? In that ye say: 'Every one that doeth evil is good in the sight of the Lord, And he delighteth in them; or where is the God of justice?'"

"....From the days of your fathers ye have turned aside from mine ordinances, and have not kept them. Return unto me and I will return unto you, saith the Lord of hosts. But ye say: 'wherein shall we return?' Will a man rob God? yet ye rob me. But ye say: 'wherein have we robbed thee?' In tithes and heave-offerings. Ye are cursed with a curse, yet ye rob me, even this whole nation."

"Bring ye the whole tithe into the store house, that there may be food in My house,and try (prove) Me now herewith, saith the Lord of hosts if I will not open the windows of heaven and pour you out a blessing, that there shall be more than sufficiency". Malachi 2:4-340 MT, KJV, JST

A temple, to be built in the future, would be laid waste and the descendants of Levi would be taken captive throughout all nations because of their wickedness. Were it not for the promises God made to Abraham, Isaac, and Israel none of Levi's descendants would be left upon the earth because of their future wickedness.

However, a Savior or Messiah would come. He would save Levi's posterity from their sins if they would repent and turn away altogether therefrom. Tragically, this Savior or Messiah would not be recognized or accepted by most of Levi's descendants. The man who renews the law in the power of the Most High God, would be called a deceiver, and at last some of Levi's descendants would rush upon Him to have him slain, not knowing His dignity, taking innocent blood through wickedness upon their own heads.

Because of what they would do to Him, they the posterity, of Levi, would be a curse among the Gentiles, and be dispersed throughout them until He (the Messiah) shall come again and visit them in pity through faith and water.

In the day the Lord sets forth His hand a second time to recover his ancient covenant people, Israel, the spirit of the Lord shall shine forth as the sun on the earth, and shall remove all darkness from under heaven, and there shall be peace in all the earth. The heavens shall exult in His days,and the earth shall be glad, and the knowledge of the Lord shall be poured forth upon the earth as the waters of the seas. The angels of glory of the presence of the Lord shall be glad in

Him. And there shall be none succeed Him for all generations to come. And in His priesthood the Gentiles shall be multiplied in knowledge upon the earth and be enlightened. In His priesthood shall sin come to an end, and the lawless shall cease to do evil.

And he shall open the gates of paradise, and shall remove the threatening sword against Adam, and he shall give His followers to eat from the tree of life, and the spirit of holiness shall be on them. And Satan shall be bound by Him, and He shall give power to His children to tread upon evil spirits. And the Lord shall rejoice in His children, and be well pleased to His beloved ones forever. Then shall Abraham, Isaac and Israel exult, and all His followers shall clothe themselves in glory.

Closing this great fore shadowing of the future Levi challenged his children to choose for themselves either light or darkness,the law of the Lord or the works of Satan. They responded by declaring they would walk before the Lord and His law. So be it, declared Levi, as the Lord's witness, His angels as witnesses, and as he Levi was witness, and as they, his sons, were witnesses.

Levi closed his life after one hundred thirty seven years. They laid him in a coffin and afterwards buried him in Hebron with Abraham, Isaac and Israel.[314]

For a more complete description, see The Testament of Levi in The Forgotten Books of Eden p. 226-233, The Old Testament Pseudepigrapha I p. 788-795, and the Ascension of Levi in the Legends of the Jews II p. 194-198.

---

314. Testament of Levi p. 226-233

Epilogue

While the scriptures contain limited information about them, other writings amplify the character, works and teachings of The Twelve Covenant Sons of Israel. Perhaps they were not as great as Abraham, Isaac, and Israel. None the less, they were great men. Some if not all, were servants and prophets of God with important messages for all mankind.

Making many errors, transgressing the laws of God at times, and committing serious sin, the sons of Israel eventually repented, rose above their humanity, and became more perfect during their lives. They learned that when they lived His laws they prospered, grew in mind and spirit, happiness and joy, reaping the benefits and blessings of God. When they transgressed His laws, broke His commandments, and otherwise sinned, they reaped the consequences in anguish, guilt, pain, punishment, and denial of God's blessings.

Jehovah announced generations earlier His work and glory is to bring to pass the immortality of all mankind, and to make possible eternal life for all who would be obedient, keep His commandments and strive for perfection. The standard of perfection for all who would seek eternal life was known to Abraham, Isaac, and Israel, and even to Noah of an earlier dispensation whom the Lord declared was "a just man and perfect in his generations, and Noah walked with God."

Noah was a covenant son of Lamech through the loins of Methuselah and Enoch, who also, were servants and prophets of God. His work and glory having been made clear, the Lord, none the less, would not preempt any man or woman's agency to choose how s/he would behave during his/her life on this earth.

As His covenant people grew in number He delegated powers to them to act for Him and to assist Him in bringing the benefits and blessings of eternal life to all mankind.

The human family born into the world were taking physical bodies in which to house spiritual bodies they received in heaven before coming to earth. Obtaining physical bodies in which to house their spiritual bodies was a blessing received from God the Eternal Father, for the choices they made and the lives they lived while spirits in the pre-mortal world. Some spirits were/are greater than others, and Jehovah was/is the greatest spiritual son of all of God the Eternal Father's (Elohim's) children.

Jehovah reemphasized this teaching through the dreams given to Joseph when he was a young lad. Joseph was to be elevated above his brethren to help achieve God's purposes. However, there were many lessons to be learned by all of Israel's family in the process.

They learned that selfishness, pride, hate, envy, jealousy, licentiousness, haughtiness, anger, self aggrandizement, and compulsion were to be replaced with selflessness, humility, love, generousity, compassion, patience, chastity, self control, personal righteousness, and persuasion. They learned that to walk uprightly before the Lord and be perfect meant their lives would have to be upgraded and improved, and were to be ones of sacrifice, service, and consecration of self to a higher cause. Such goals and the achievement of them demonstrate worthiness to receive God's blessings; leads to true happiness, a fullness of joy and to eternal life.

They learned what it means to repent, and to turn altogether away from their sins. They learned the vital role of forgiveness of others, as a means of receiving forgiveness from God for their own sins, and the importance of unfeigned love for one another. They learned that failure to forgive those who trespassed against them cankered their own souls and nearly destroyed them.

They learned to exercise faith in the Lord, to pray to Him and to be obedient to Him. They learned that God the Eternal Father would send a perfect one without spot or blemish who would take a body and live among men, who would take upon Himself the sins of all mankind and would pay for them with His own life, that all mankind might be saved from their own sins through repentance.

They learned that they were accountable for their own sins and not for Adam's transgression.

Tempted, tried, and proven in the refiners fire, Joseph was elevated above the people of Egypt, and above his brethren. The Pharaoh was so impressed he gave Joseph a new name Zaphenath-paneah, which stood for seer, redeemer, prophet, supporter, interpreter of dreams, clever, discreet, wise and revealer of secrets.

The Pharaoh and the Lord did not agree on many issues. On this issue they agreed: Joseph, son of Israel was a prophet, seer, and revelator, acting in behalf of the Lord. Israel apparently ordained Joseph a prophet, seer, and revelator when he conferred upon him the birthright blessing. Joseph's teenage dreams of sheaves of grain and of stars making obeisance were prophesies of future events. He served as a prophet, seer and revelator until his death.

His future descendents through Manasseh would write the stick of Joseph, which was to be joined with the stick of Judah for the edification and salvation of future generations. This scripture would be revealed to the world as part of the fullness of the Gospel when it is restored by Joseph's descendents through Ephraim. The name Ephraim means restored, according to the Antiquities of the Jews. It is through Ephraim's posterity the truth as it was known in Abraham's, Isaac's, Israel's and Joseph's day, is being restored in our day, according to the Latter Day Saints.

Principles taught by the twelve sons of Israel in their day strike a responsive chord in the hearts of Latter Day Saints in our day. Latter Day Saints believe and teach many of the same principles.

Some choice morsels from the twelve sons of Israel:

From Joseph:

> "If you pursue self control and purity with patience and prayer with fasting in humility in heart, the Lord will dwell among you, because he loves self control."

> "For God loveth him who in a den of wickedness combines fasting with chastity, rather than the man who in king's chambers combines

luxury with license."

"....if ye follow after chastity and purity with patience and prayer, with fasting in humility in heart, the Lord will dwell among you because he loveth chastity. And wheresoever the Most High dwelleth, even though envy,or slavery, or slander befalleth a man, the Lord dwelleth in him, for the sake of his chastity, not only delivereth him from evil, but also exalteth him, even as me, For in every way the man is lifted up, whether in deed or in word or in thought."

"For everyone who doeth the law of the Lord shall be loved by him."

"Love one another, and with long suffering hide ye one another's faults."

"For God delighteth in the unity of brethren, and in the purpose of a heart that takes pleasure in love."

"I exalted not myself among them in arrogance because of my worldly glory, but I was among them as one of the least."

"If ye also, therefore, walk in the commandments of the Lord, my children, He will exalt you there, and will bless you with good things forever and ever. And if any one seeketh to do evil unto you, do well with him, and pray for him, and ye shall be redeemed of the Lord from all evil."

From Zebulun:

Zebulun counseled his children to keep the commands of God and to show mercy to their neighbors, to have compassion towards all, both to humans and to beasts. He related his own experiences in providing compassionate service when his brethren were sick, saying:

"even as man doeth to his neighbor, even so will the Lord do to him."

He broiled fish, dressed them and offered them to men in need or to those grieving, explaining:

"he that shareth with his neighbor, receiveth manifold more from the Lord."

Zebulun counseled his children not to hesitate in showing compassion and mercy to all saying:

"For in the degree in which a man hath compassion upon his neighbours, in the same degree hath the Lord also upon him."

From Simeon:

"....beware of the spirit of deceit and envy. For envy ruleth over the whole mind of man....it ever suggesteth to him to destroyeth him that envieth; and so long as he that is envied flouresheth, he that envieth fadeth away."

Having had first hand experience with envy and jealousy, Simeon said these two cause anger and war in the mind and stirs up deeds of blood, leading the mind into frenzy, causing tumult of the soul and trembling of the body. Even in sleep malicious jealousy gnaws on the soul, causes the body to be troubled, and awakens the mind from sleep in confusion. Simeon counselled his children to be aware of fornication calling it the mother of all evils, which separates those who commit fornication from God and brings them to Satan.

From Reuben:

Reuben counselled his children not to walk in the sins of youth and fornication as he had done when he defiled his father's bed. He said that fornication had destroyed many a man though he be young or old, noble or rich or poor. A man who commits fornication brings reproach to himself and allows himself to be controlled by Satan. Reuben assured his sons that Satan could not overcome them if they would not yield to fornication. He counselled his daughters not to use their wiles to seduce men. He adjured them to be truthful with one another and with their neighbors and to love one another.

From Dan:

Dan counselled his children to keep themselves from the spirit of lying and anger, to love truth and long suffering instead. They should observe the commandments of God, keep His law, speak the truth, love the Lord and one another with a true heart.

The children of Dan were encouraged to draw near unto God (the Eternal Father) and unto the angel of peace (His Son) that intercedeth for them. "Depart, therefore, from all unrighteousness, and cleave unto the righteousness of God...."

From Issachar:

Issachar apparently did not seek power or glory or the vain things of life. He counselled his children to not show envy, evil, and maliciousness; to work in guilelessness, to love the Lord and their neighbors; and to have compassion on the poor and the weak. He encouraged them to toil in the labors of the field, to offer the first fruits of the earth to God and He, the Lord God, would bless them as He had blessed all His followers from Abel until "now."

Issachar declared he had been true to his wife, had not drunk wine, or coveted anything of his neighbors. He had not lied, nor had guile arose in his heart. He had shared his bread with the poor, had loved the Lord and every man. He counselled his children to do likewise.

From Asher:

Asher explained that when a soul departs this life troubled, it is tormented by the evil spirit it served in lust and evil work. On the other hand, the soul that departs in peace, meets the angel of peace (the Savior or Messiah) who leads him/her to eternal life.

From Gad:

Gad encouraged his children to hearken to the words of truth, to work righteousness, to live all the law of the Most High God, and not go astray through the spirit of hatred, for hatred, said he, is evil in all the doings of men. Gad said that those filled with hate despise the truth, envy those who prosper, welcomes evil speaking, and loves arrogance. Hatred, said he, blinds the soul. When filled with hatred, a man will not hear the words of God's commandments concerning the love of ones neighbors; for he delights in reporting to others those who stumble, and is quick to demand judgement and punishment for those who have stumbled.

He contrasted love with hatred, saying that as love would quicken even the dead, and would call back them that are condemned to die, so hatred would slay the living, and those who have sinned venially, it would not suffer to live. The spirit of hatred works with Satan and death, while the spirit of love working with the law of God in long suffering brings about the salvation of men.

Gad said he was speaking from his own experience with hatred, which was of the devil, and urged his children to cleave to the love of God. He said righteousness casts out hatred and humility destroys envy. He that is just and humble is ashamed to do what is unjust, being reproved not of another, but of his own heart. He speaks not against a holy man, because the love of God overcomes hatred. He would not wrong any man, not even in thought.

Gad said it took him a lifetime to learn these lessons and that he had repented of his thoughts and actions concerning Joseph. Repentance, said Gad, destroys ignorance, drives away darkness, enlightens the eyes, gives knowledge to the soul, and leads the mind to salvation. He counselled his children to love one another in deed and in word, and to put away hatred from their hearts. He urged them to be forgiving of those who transgress against them.

From Naphtali:

Naphtali encouraged his children to work that which is good, to be wise and prudent in understanding the order of God's commandments and His laws.

From Benjamin:

Benjamin encouraged his children to be followers of the kind of compassion Joseph had shown his brethren who had sold him, and not envy those who are glorified by God. Those valiant in following the Lord should be praised, and the virtuous lauded. His children were counselled to have mercy on the poor, to have compassion for the weak, and to sing praises unto God. Darkness flees away from him who reverences good works.

He with a pure mind in love, looks not after a woman with a view of fornication, for he has no defilement in his heart, because the spirit of God rests in him. As the sun is not defiled by shining on dung or mire, but rather dries up both and drives away the evil smell, so also the pure mind though encompassed by the defilements of earth, rather cleanses them and is not itself defiled.

Benjamin encouraged his children to keep the commandments of God, to walk in holiness and to endure to the end.

From Judah:

....The spirit of fornication has wine as a minister to give pleasure to the mind and heats up the body to carnal union. The love of money or gold dethrones the reason of man. The love of money leads to idolatry, and when led astray through money, men name as gods those things that are not Gods. Judah declared that the spirit of truth testifies all things.

From Levi:

Levi counselled his children to work righteousness upon the earth that they might have treasure in heaven, to sow good things in their souls that they might find them in their lives. He pled with them to avoid those things which would lead them astray from the Lord, declaring whosoever teaches noble things and does them, shall be enthroned with kings as was Joseph. He said that heaven is purer in the Lords sight than the earth, so also be ye the light of Israel, purer than the Gentiles.

The past and future of Israel's posterity were revealed and prophesied by his twelve sons. These revelations and prophesies enlighten our understanding of the nature of the Lord God Jehovah, and the nature of Israel's forebears and posterity, the Lord's covenant people through whom He works to achieve His purposes.

The origins of Jehovah's spiritual body and the spiritual bodies of all mankind had been revealed generations earlier in Abraham's day and were apparently recognized by all Israel. Jehovah and all of mankind have a Father in Heaven: His name is Elohim.

As the spiritual bodies of Adam, Eve and all that followed from their union until the days of Israel, and his twelve sons, had been enveloped in flesh, so was the spiritual body of Jehovah to be enveloped in flesh sometime in the future. As prophets, seers and revelators had been raised up in the past to help Him, so would others be raised up in the future to help bring about the eternal life of men and women.

Several of Israel's sons prophesied that the lineage of Jehovah in the flesh would be through the loins of Judah and of Levi.

Before Jehovah would be made flesh, however, the children of Israel would fall into idolatry and be enslaved by the Egyptians. They would have to be retaught that which their forebears knew.

Under the leadership of Judah, the children of Israel were saved from physical destruction as they battled the Canaanite kings. Under the leadership of Joseph the children of Israel were saved from the famine of food. Under the leadership of Moses, a descendant of Levi, the children of Israel would later be saved from slavery and idolatry. The Messiah or Savior would come in the future to save Israel and all mankind from the bonds of physical death and to make possible salvation from spiritual death. All mankind might be saved from their sins provided they would walk uprightly before Him and perfect themselves through repentance.

Though prophets, seers, and revelators wrought miracles in behalf of God in the battles against warring nations, against the famine of food, and against slavery and idolatry, no prophet, seer or revelator had been given power to break the bonds of death, or to save the children of Israel and of all mankind from their sins. Redemption from physical and spiritual death would come through Jehovah, the son of God the Eternal Father Himself.

Someone without sin, blemish or spot would be needed to undertake this great assignment, symbolized by the law of sacrifice introduced to Adam by the Lord and continued during the days of Abel and Cain, reintroduced in the days of Noah, and again in the days of Abraham, Isaac and Israel. Our Heavenly Father required the first and best of offerings whether they be lambs, or birds or grain of Israel, in similitude of the offering of His own, first born Son, Jehovah who had been born to Him in the spirit but had not yet been born in the flesh.

No one yet born in the flesh was qualified, to whom God the Eternal Father could give power to break the bonds of physical and spiritual death, redeem all mankind and bring them back into His presence. All Israel and all the world had sinned, all needed to repent, all needed to be forgiven, and all needed to be reconciled with their Eternal Father.

Joseph, son of Israel, reportedly saw the future birth of the Messiah who would come through the loins of Judah, whom he declared would be as a lamb without spot. Zebulun referred to the Lord as the light of righteousness. Simeon declared the coming of a mighty one of Israel who would take a body and eat with men. He would be as an High Priest and a King of the loins of both Levi and Judah. He would come to save all Israel and all the Gentiles as well, from their sins. Dan apparently declared this Savior to come was to be the Savior of all mankind, and He was/is to serve as a mediator between God the Eternal Father and mankind. Asher prophesied that the Most High (God) would come Himself as man, eating and drinking, with power greater than Satan's. Gad prophesied that from Levi and Judah's posterity salvation would come to Israel.

Benjamin declared that a blameless one, a Lamb of God would be sent to save all Israel and all the world from the sins of its people. As Joseph was initially rejected by his brethren, scorned and sold, so would this blameless one be initially rejected, sold and delivered unto the hands of lawless men. This blameless one would die for ungodly men in the blood of the covenant for the salvation of the Gentiles as well as all Israel. As Joseph later forgave his brethren, so this blameless one, even the Savior, the Son of God, the Messiah, would forgive those who rejected Him and scorned Him, if they repent.

Naphtali reportedly said that the Lord made the physical body of man after the likeness of the body of man's spirit, one perfectly fitting the other, and that God created every man after His own image. He also declared that God knows men and women, and how far each will persist in goodness or evil. No two men or two women were made exactly alike. Each was and is a unique creation of God.

Before the coming of Jehovah in the flesh, however, many other events were to transpire. The children of Israel were to learn many lessons before that day was to come.

The sons of Israel saw the future of their posterity, in part. They prophesied concerning their future afflictions in Egypt, their deliverance from those afflictions through a future prophet whom both Israel and Joseph declared would be called Moses.

They saw the division of the children of Israel into two kingdoms, and their subsequent scattering to the ends of the earth.

They saw the future writing of scriptures by the descendants of Judah and of Joseph, both having been commanded of God to be written, which would later be used to bring salvation to all of mankind. They saw the future coming of the Messiah, even the Lord God Jehovah, who would be enveloped in flesh, with power to break the bonds of physical and spiritual death.

A New Jerusalem was to be built in the last days near Eden. Some of the children of Israel would be gathered there. Others would gather to the land of promise in the old Jerusalem as they had prophesied. Ye children of Israel in our day shall we not accept Levi's challenge: As heaven is purer in the Lord's sight than the earth, so be we as the light of Israel, purer than the Gentiles, letting personal righteousness be the guiding principle of our lives, that we may lead them to, and do the will of Him whom Isaiah declared shall be called, Wonderful, Counselor, The Mighty God, the Everlasting Father, and the Prince of Peace. Isaiah 9:6 (Pele-Joez-el-gibber-Abi-ad-Sar-Shalom, That is Wonderful in Counsel is God the Mighty, the everlasting Father, the Ruler of Peace).

(Note)

These themes were begun in a previous work entitled "ABRAHAM, ISAAC, AND JACOB, SERVANTS AND PROPHETS OF GOD," tracing Abraham, Isaac's and Jacob's posterity through the Twelve Sons of Israel in the work just finished. Future works will trace the children of Israel through Moses, Aaron, Ephraim, Manasseh and Joshua; David, Solomon, Daniel, Isaiah, Ezekiel, Elijah, Malachi, Lehi, Nephi, Mosiah, Abinadi, Alma, Helaman, Mormon, Moroni, Jared, his brother and others.

Sources for these works include those books God has caused to be written for he said, "For I command all men both in the east and in the west, and in the north, and in the south, and in the islands of the sea, that they shall write the words which I speak unto them; for out of the books which shall be written I will judge the world, every man according to their (his) works according to that which is written." Book of Mormon (2Nephi 29:11)

BIBLIOGRAPHY

1. The Holy Bible, Authorized King James Version, Old & New Testaments, The Church of Jesus Christ of Latter Day Saints, Salt Lake City, 1979.

2. The Holy Scriptures, According To The Masoretic Text, The Jewish Publication Society of America, Philadelphia, 1955.

3. The Holy Scriptures Containing The Old & New Testaments, Board of Publication of The Reorganized Church of Jesus Christ of Latter Day Saints, Independence, Tenth Printing, 1964.

4. Charlesworth, James H., The Old Testament Pseudepigrapha Volume, 1, Testaments of the Twelve Patriarchs (Second Century BC) p 782-828 Doubleday & Company, Inc., Garden City, 1983.

5. The Forgotten Books of Eden The Testaments of the Twelve Patriarchs p 220-269 World Bible Publishers Inc. 1927.

6. Ginzberg, Louis, The Legends of the Jews, Philadelphia, The Jewish Publication Society of America (7 volumes), 1910.

7. Smith, Joseph, Jr. Translator, The Book of Mormon, The Church of Jesus Christ of Latter Day Saints, Salt Lake City, 1977.

8. Smith, Joseph Jr., The Pearl of Great Price, A Selection the Revelations, Translations, and Narrations of Joseph Smith - Book of Abraham, The Church of Jesus Christ of Latter Day Saints, Salt Lake City, 1974.

9. Smith, Joseph Jr., Prophet, Seer & Revelator, The Doctrine and Covenants, The Church of Jesus Christ of Latter Day Saints, Salt Lake City, 1979.

10. The Book of Jasher, J.H. Parry Company, Salt Lake City, 1887, 1973.

11. The Antiquities of the Jews, Complete Works of Flavius Josephus, Whiston, William Translator, Kregel Publications, Grand Rapids 1978.